Rachel Khoo's Kitchen Notebook

over 100 delicious recipes
from my personal cookbook

Photography by David Loftus
Illustrations by Rachel Khoo

Michael Joseph an imprint of Penguin Books

MICHAEL JOSEPH

Published by the Penguin Group

Penguin Books Ltd, 80 Strand, London WC2R 0RL, England

Penguin Group (USA) Inc., 375 Hudson Street, New York, New York 10014, USA

Penguin Group (Canada), 90 Eglinton Avenue East, Suite 700, Toronto, Ontario, Canada M4P 2YR
(a division of Pearson Penguin Canada Inc.)

Penguin Ireland, 25 St Stephen's Green, Dublin 2, Ireland (a division of Penguin Books Ltd)

Penguin Group (Australia), 707 Collins Street, Melbourne, Victoria 3008, Australia
(a division of Pearson Australia Group Pty Ltd)

Penguin Books India Pvt Ltd, 11 Community Centre, Panchsheel Park, New Delhi – 110 017, India

Penguin Group (NZ), 67 Apollo Drive, Rosedale, Auckland 0632, New Zealand
(a division of Pearson New Zealand Ltd)

Penguin Books (South Africa) (Pty) Ltd, Block D, Rosebank Office Park, 181 Jan Smuts Avenue,
Parktown North, Gauteng 2193, South Africa

Penguin Books Ltd, Registered Offices: 80 Strand, London WC2R 0RL, England

www.penguin.com

www.rachelkhoo.com

First published 2015

001

Text copyright © Rachel Khoo, 2015

Photography copyright © David Loftus, 2015

Illustrations copyright © Peas in a Pot Ltd, 2015

Set in Gill Sans and Trixie

Printed in China

A CIP catalogue record for this book is available from the British Library

ISBN: 978–0–718–17946–5

Penguin
Random
House

Contents

Introduction

I carry a notebook everywhere, and it almost always ends up tattered, dog-eared and splashed with various food stains from eating my way around the world or cooking in my kitchen. The recipes, illustrations, kitchen titbits and tips that end up in my notebook are all something that I wanted to share. Recipes that reflect both my culinary past and my present, the places I've been, my kitchen experiences . . . a book that tells a story of how I cook in the kitchen.

After writing two cookbooks that chronicled my exploration of *la cuisine française*, I felt it was time to show my true colours with this book. My childhood played a big part in forming my culinary DNA, but the experiences and cultures I've exposed myself to in my adult life have also been formative in the way my cooking style has evolved. The last several years have been packed tighter than a tin of sardines with adventures close to home and beyond. I've visited an eclectic range of places, from the Scandi-cool Stockholm and the fragrant delights of the East in Istanbul, to the slightly rough-around-the-edges Naples, as well as rediscovering my home town, London, with its vibrant, energetic food scene.

Even though I've lived in Paris for eight years, I am not 'that French woman off the telly', as I've frequently been described since the *Little Paris Kitchen* TV show aired. I'm quite proudly British (despite the many years of British food bashing I endured in France), with a colourful culinary heritage, thanks to my Malaysian dad and Austrian mum. Living in Bavaria as a teenager has also played its part. My taste buds were stimulated from a young age with spices, flavours and smells from South-East Asia, sweet and heart-warming dishes from Austria, as well as some British classics like roast beef and Yorkshire puddings. Although I had a diverse culinary upbringing, my parents were not snobby when it came to food. They understood the importance of nutritious home-cooked food and the ritual of sitting down for a meal every day as a family, but the odd fast food treat or TV dinner was still allowed. My mum has always been a savvy shopper, never wasting a thing and ever-inventive with leftovers. Our so-called 'leftovers night', a common thing at home, would often look like the foodie equivalent of a United Colours of Benetton commercial, with schnitzel, shepherd's pie, rendang curry and stir-fried rice all on the table at the same time. When I look back, I think my parents were unintended foodie visionaries with their leftover fusion food. Eating Austrian dumpling soup with some char siu roasted pork and pickled chillies was not unusual in the Khoo household, and this was back in the eighties, long before Korean tacos or kebab pizza were the norm.

I come from a creative background. I spent four years at art college, working on projects where the main objective was to communicate an idea through a particular medium,

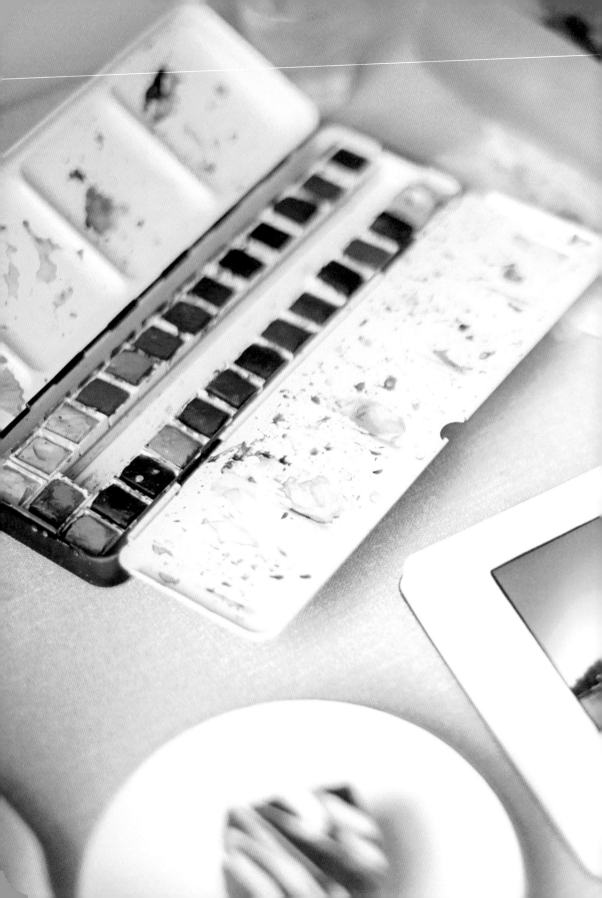

in my case graphic/web design and photography. I was initially drawn to food because it's a way of expressing my creativity with an added tasty bonus. Since I started writing cookbooks, I feel like I have hit the jackpot. It combines many of my passions: creativity, socializing and eating!

The way I go about creating a recipe book is similar to the creative practice I learnt at art college. Just like an art project, it all starts with hands-on research, initial ideas scribbled in my notebook, which evolve into experiments and then the final piece. I like to travel, to meet people, to experience the food, the culture, the flavours, sights, sounds and smells first-hand, gathering the inspiration and research to feed my brain and tummy with ideas. Those ideas end up being an initial scribble and sketch in my notebook. Then, when it comes to taking the sketch from concept to recipe creation, chaos ensues in the kitchen, with pots, pans and many ingredients being thrown around. More often than not, the recipe does not turn out quite the way I imagined on paper. However, even the failures are usually successes: I might discover a new flavour combination, or texture, or cooking technique. If it's really a total disaster, it ultimately helps me to write a better recipe, as I'll then understand better what can go wrong in the kitchen. I always believe that failures are part of the process. It's how you deal with them that will eventually influence whether you succeed or not.

The famous communication philosopher Marshall McLuhan once said that 'the medium is the message'. A cookbook has a tactile and personal element that a recipe on a tablet or TV show can't have. Reading a tablet in the bathtub is a little more risky than reading a book. But this goes beyond the physical object for me. I think of a recipe as a little snapshot of what I've experienced, and putting them together in a book is like collating a personal culinary diary.

It's a time-consuming process, but I love every part of it, from the research, recipe development and writing about my personal stories, to the photo shoot, where the book begins to take a visual shape. Writing a book may start off as a solitary activity, but the more the book progresses, the more essential it is to work with people you admire and find inspiring (more about them in the Acknowledgements). They all play a part in pushing me as a food writer and making the book the best it can be.

My ideas start with a taste, a flavour and a sketch in my kitchen notebook, then evolve from experiments in my kitchen back into the book and eventually (I hope!) to your kitchen and your mouths. My culinary holy grail is to find my cookbook on your bookshelf with greasy fingerprints, food-stain splatters and your own personal scribbles on the recipes.

This book is a collection of recipes that were inspired by my travels, adventures and food experiences, which I hope, ultimately, inspire you to cook!

Rachel x

Cream of tomato soup with crunchy lemon chickpeas

Starters

Olive Oil

Light bites or small dishes to tantalize your taste buds: that's what starters are all about. More often than not they set a tone, showing your guests what culinary delights await them and giving them a little taste of what's in store. Starters also make a fantastic meal for one or two – see my little socca cakes with ratatouille (page 33) or my hot butter and soy sauce mackerel with chopped salad (page 41). I often opt for a selection of starters rather than one main course when I eat out. I'm never happy with just one plate of food; I like to try lots of different things – and with small dishes I can leave the restaurant without feeling like I need a forklift truck to take me home. Since I began developing recipes for a living, I often also find myself having a starter as a lunch or light dinner, and sometimes even for breakfast . . . or perhaps that's just my Asian heritage coming to light.

Starters aren't just reserved for special occasions. On the Continent it is perfectly normal, and totally sensible in my mind, to kick off a home meal – guests or no guests, mid-week or brunch – with a little appetite whetter; it's a great way of prolonging time spent at the table too. When I cooked for a French family, I discovered that a starter can simply be a slice of perfectly ripe melon with a few ribbons of salty, sweet Bayonne ham. For some other easy, quick starters, see my poached fennel with pink prawns and toasted almonds (page 38), pan con tomate (page 25) or the rather unusual morcilla, egg and crisps (page 25).

I don't believe you need to serve something complex in order to wow your guests, but if you're looking to push the boat out then some of my favourites are my ultra-bling smörgåstårta (page 57) or my dainty baked goat's cheese cigars with melon, radish and cucumber slaw (page 21).

And if you're new to the kitchen, or have a tendency to burn your food, I even have a recipe for you too: my burnt leek parcels with romesco sauce (page 34). It's one of those few recipes in which burning your food is not so much undesirable as a sought-after outcome.

Creamy mushroom soup with bouncy dill fish balls

Serves 4 (makes 1 litre of soup)	Preparation time: 25 minutes	Cooking time: 30 minutes

The archipelago around Stockholm, with its crystal-clear water, crisp fresh air and untouched scenery, captured what for me is the essence of Sweden. It is the juxtaposition of water and forest that inspired this recipe, and, of course, the Swedes' love of meatballs. I turned tradition on its head a little, and let the coast inspire these fish balls. But these aren't just any old fish balls.

Instead of taking the more traditional Swedish approach to making meatballs (ground meat or fish, rolled into a ball), I've taken inspiration from my Chinese heritage. I love the chewy texture of Chinese fish balls, which is created by slapping the flesh around. I've spotted old ladies in fish markets in Malaysia doing this. The pounding and slamming of the fish stretches and uncoils the previously wound protein strands, which makes for this unusual bouncy texture.

For the soup

1 tbsp olive oil

2 knobs of butter

2 onions, peeled and finely chopped

2 cloves of garlic, peeled and minced

2 sprigs of thyme

500g portobello mushrooms, roughly chopped

sea salt and freshly ground pepper

500ml good-quality beef or chicken stock

300ml single cream

zest and juice of 1 unwaxed lemon

For the fish balls (makes 16)

400g cod or pollack loin, skinned and deboned

2 tbsp chopped fresh dill, plus extra to garnish

½ tsp sea salt

¼ tsp white pepper

50ml water

For the topping

60g wild mushrooms (such as chanterelles, girolles or pied de mouton), brushed, torn if large

1 knob of butter

2–3 knäckebröd, or rye crispbread

Heat the oil and butter in a large pan, add the onions, garlic, sprigs of thyme and mushrooms, then season with salt and pepper and cook uncovered on a low heat for 15 minutes, or until soft.

In the meantime, prepare the fish balls. Pat the fish dry with kitchen towel. In a food processor, blend the fish to a smooth paste with the dill, salt and pepper. Add about 40ml of the water and keep blending. Check the consistency and add as much water as needed to bind into a paste; you want it to be paste-like but not too wet to form into balls.

Now it's time to start slapping your fish. Take the mixture in your hands and keep slapping it down on a clean work surface, for a minute or two. As the mixture is thrown down more and more, you will notice a bounce develop in the texture.

Divide the mixture into 16 and shape into small balls. If you find it easier, wet your palms before rolling the mixture into neat balls. Place on a clean plate.

Add the stock to your mushrooms and leave to simmer for a further 10 minutes, uncovered. Add the cream. Remove and discard the thyme stalks and whizz up the soup with a hand blender.

Fill a medium saucepan with water, bring it to the boil and drop the fish balls in to cook for 3 minutes, or until they float to the top. Remove with a slotted spoon and set aside. Fry the wild mushrooms in a frying pan with the butter for 2–3 minutes, then set aside.

Finish off the soup by stirring in the lemon juice and tasting for seasoning. Divide the soup between bowls, adding 4 fish balls to each. Garnish with some shards of knäckebröd as croutons, some fresh dill and lemon zest. Scatter some of the sautéed wild mushrooms on top of each bowl.

Tip

Soak the bowl of your blender or food processor immediately after making the fish paste, as it has a tendency to stick!

Get ahead

You can make the soup a day before. The fish balls can be formed the day before serving, store in an airtight container and cook just before serving.

Cream of tomato soup with crunchy lemon chickpeas

Serves 4 as a starter	Preparation time: 15 minutes	Cooking time: 35–45 minutes

Anyone who has ever cooked and eaten on a budget in the UK will be familiar with some of Britain's perennial foodstuffs: tins of canned soup and tomatoey baked beans. They were the standby meals of choice back in my uni days, and there is nothing quite like a cream of tomato soup to brighten up a winter night.

I love these lemony chickpeas (I always have a tin of chickpeas to hand in the cupboard): my version of croutons. I like to sprinkle them on top of soups, but they are equally delicious as a stand in for nuts – a homemade bar snack.

1 x 400g tin of chickpeas, drained and rinsed (drained weight 240g)

1 unwaxed lemon, sliced

4 cloves of garlic, unpeeled

1 tbsp rapeseed or other vegetable oil

sea salt

2 x 400g tins of good-quality cherry tomatoes

250ml vegetable stock or water

1 tsp sugar

1 tbsp red wine vinegar

freshly ground pepper

200ml single cream

Preheat the oven to 180°C (fan).

Toss the chickpeas, lemon and garlic in the oil and place on a baking tray. Sprinkle with salt and roast for 30– 40 minutes, or until golden and crunchy.

In the meantime, put the tomatoes and vegetable stock or water into a medium saucepan and bring to a simmer. Remove the roasted garlic from the baking tray and squeeze the garlic from its skin, then add to the saucepan and simmer for 5 minutes. Add the sugar and vinegar and continue simmering for 1 minute. Taste for seasoning and stir in half of the cream, then remove from the heat and blend until smooth with a hand blender.

Ladle the soup into bowls and garnish each with the crunchy chickpeas, a slice of roasted lemon and a drizzle of cream.

Tips
Don't boil the soup with the cream in it, as it will curdle.

Baked goat's cheese cigars with melon, radish and cucumber slaw

Serves
4 as a starter

Preparation time:
20 minutes

Cooking time:
15–20 minutes

The Nice area tends to produce goat's cheese rather than cheese made from cow's milk, as the landscape is too rugged and rough for cows to graze. Eating goat's cheese from this region really captures the flavours of the terroir. Goats graze on whatever grows, from wild herbs like oregano and thyme to berries, and these flavours subtly influence the end product. These make a delectable summer starter or an aperitif with a glass of rosé, showcasing the flavours of Provence.

1–2 rectangular filo sheets (depending on the size of your sheets)

60g butter, melted

8 sprigs of thyme, leaves picked

125g soft goat's cheese

4 tsp honey (lavender if possible)

For the slaw

1 small cucumber or ½ a regular cucumber

½ unripe galia melon, seeds removed

6 radishes, trimmed and sliced into thin rounds

For the dressing

1 tbsp extra virgin olive oil

½ tbsp red wine vinegar

sea salt and freshly ground pepper, to taste

Preheat the oven to 180°C (fan).

Unroll a sheet of filo horizontally on your work surface. Cut the filo sheet in half lengthways and in half crossways to make 4 rectangles measuring approximately 15cm x 20cm. Lay them all out on the work surface, then brush the rectangles generously with butter, ensuring that about 1 tablespoon is saved to brush the tops.

Sprinkle some thyme leaves along the long length of each pastry rectangle and fold it in about 2cm to encase them. Crumble a line of goat's cheese in a line along the opposite short side of the pastry. Drizzle the honey along the goat's cheese on each pastry. Starting at the goat's cheese end, roll the pastry over the cheese and all way to the thyme, sealing the join. Repeat the process to make 4 cigars.

Place on a lined baking tray and brush again with the remaining butter. Bake for 15–20 minutes, or until golden and crisp.

In the meantime, make the salad by using a mandolin or speed peeler to julienne the cucumber and the melon flesh. Place them all in a bowl with the radishes. Put the dressing ingredients into a small bowl or jam jar and mix well.

Once the cigars are cooked, toss your salad with the dressing and place in the centre of your plate. Serve with the cigars on top.

Tips

Filo sheets dry out really quickly. Be sure to store them in cling film. Be gentle when brushing the sheets as they can tear easily.

You can flavour the goat's cheese with any dried herbs or spices, for example cayenne pepper, smoked paprika, ground cumin or chilli, also try a spoonful of your favourite chutney or caramelized onions in place of the honey.

Speedy chorizo and chickpea stew

Serves	Preparation time:	Cooking time:
4–6 as a starter or 2 as a main	10 minutes	20 minutes

One of the great things about tapas is that they can be whipped up in a flash. This speedy little stew is at home on a table laden down with a selection of tapas, or serve it for two and have a tasty meal in minutes.

8 spring onions

1 tbsp olive oil

1 tbsp finely chopped fresh rosemary leaves

1 tsp smoked sweet paprika

400g tin of cooked chickpeas, drained and rinsed (drained weight 250g)

2 chorizo cooking sausages

1 × 400g tin of cherry tomatoes

2 tbsp sherry vinegar

Chop the spring onions into rounds, separating the white and green parts. Put the oil into a large frying pan over a high heat. Add the white part of the spring onions, the rosemary, smoked paprika and chickpeas to the pan and fry for 2 minutes.

Slice the chorizo into 1cm rounds, add to the pan and cook for 2 minutes. Add the sherry vinegar, turn down the heat and cook gently, uncovered, for a further 5 minutes, stirring occasionally.

Add the tinned tomatoes and cook for a further 10 minutes. Taste for seasoning, and adjust if necessary.

Finish the stew off with the green tops of the spring onions, just before serving.

Morcilla, egg and crisps

Serves	Preparation time:	Cooking time:
4	2 minutes	10 minutes

OK, so it sounds a little out there, but this tasty tapa is not as crazy as you might think. Unlike the British relationship with crisps, where we might stop by the corner shop for a sneaky bag of Walker's, there's a long-standing tradition of handmade, freshly fried crisps in Spain. I ate this dish in a tapas bar in Barcelona; I loved the idea that you can pimp up a bag of crisps, so I have recreated it here.

100g bag of ready-salted crisps

150g morcilla, skin removed

1 tbsp olive or rapeseed oil

3 eggs

Empty your bag of crisps into a serving dish.

Roughly crumble or chop the morcilla. Heat a large non-stick frying pan and dry-fry the morcilla for 3–4 minutes before scattering it over the crisps.

Add the oil to the frying pan, heat, and crack the eggs in one by one. Cook for 2–3 minutes, until the white is set but the yolk is still runny (put a lid or plate over the pan to speed it up).

Place the fried eggs over the morcilla and break them up with your fork to eat.

Pan con tomate

Serves	Preparation time:	Cooking time:
4	10 minutes	5 minutes

This is my take on the classic tomato on bread that is ubiquitous in Spanish wine and tapas bars. This is possibly one of the simplest tapas you'll find, but I have jazzed mine up with a herby and garlicky butter.

4 large slices of sourdough bread

300g heritage tomatoes

40g fresh basil, leaves and stalks (or whatever herbs you like)

2 cloves of garlic, peeled

80g salted butter

sea salt and freshly ground pepper

optional: a pinch of sweet smoked paprika

Grill or toast the bread on both sides. Thinly slice the tomatoes.

In a small blender or by hand, very finely chop the herbs and garlic and mix together. Melt the butter in a pan and add the herbs and garlic to it. Add a pinch of salt and pepper, and remove from the heat before the butter browns.

Pile the tomatoes high on to the toasted bread and drizzle with the hot garlic and herb butter. Finish with a sprinkle of sweet smoked paprika (if using).

A couple of small plates of food and a bunch of friends is my favourite way to rela

Razor clams with tzatziki and pomegranate

Serves
4 as a canapé or starter

Preparation time:
10 minutes

Cooking time:
30 seconds

Whenever there are mezze being served in Turkey, a small dish of tzatziki is likely to appear. It's a simple blend of cucumber, garlic and creamy yoghurt, but each family and restaurant will have their own secret method and ratio, making it their signature.

In my view the perfect tzatziki is made using a crunchy Lebanese or ridge cucumber with the seeds scooped out; salting it in a colander also draws out the moisture. Pomegranate seeds are the perfect way to pimp up any dish, savoury or sweet, and they add an exceedingly satisfying crunch.

8 razor clams

½ a lemon

75g Greek yoghurt

1 small clove of garlic, peeled and minced

a pinch of sea salt

½ a Lebanese cucumber or ridge cucumber, peeled

4 tbsp pomegranate seeds

Bring a large pan of water to the boil. Set up a large bowl of iced water nearby. Drop 4 razor clams into the boiling water, then fish them out almost immediately with a pair of tongs and drop them straight into the cold water. They should open but not cook. Repeat with the remaining clams.

Pull the clams out of their shells and prep them: use a pair of scissors to cut the black sac out of the clam, remove the 'beak', then chop the clams into thumbnail-sized pieces. Put the clams into a bowl and squeeze a little lemon juice over the top. Wash and dry 8 half-shells and set aside.

Mix together the yoghurt, garlic, salt and a squeeze of lemon to taste. Place in a disposable piping bag or food bag and snip the end off.

Cut the cucumber in half lengthways and scoop out the seeds. Cut into fine julienne strips on a mandolin or by hand.

Put 2 or 3 blobs of the garlic yoghurt along a half-shell. Put the clam pieces in between the blobs of yoghurt. Garnish with a little cucumber and scatter some of the pomegranate seeds over. Repeat with the remaining half-shells.

Tip
A good way to tell if your clams are fresh is to tickle the foot, which should retract straight away; if there is no sign of life, don't buy them.

Razor clams with crispy rice and hot sauce

Serves	Preparation time:	Cooking time:
4 as a canapé or starter	30 minutes	30 minutes

On the Princes' Islands in Turkey, seafood is a staple. *Midye dolma* – mussels stuffed with rice, pine nuts, currants and spices – are sold on the beach front, and served as the inspiration for this little mezze of mine. 'Mezze' means taste, flavour, snack or relish, which is literally how these are intended to be served – as tasters, alongside other little dishes. But don't think you have to make lots of complicated dishes for a successful spread; simply using one main ingredient and varying it with some sides or garnishes is a less fussy solution. This stuffed-clam recipe pairs perfectly with the razor clams with tzatziki and pomegranate (see page 29).

50g uncooked (or 100g cooked) brown rice

8 razor clams

2 tbsp olive oil, plus extra for drizzling

1 small onion, peeled and finely chopped

4 cloves of garlic, peeled and finely minced

8 cherry tomatoes, roughly chopped

1 small red chilli, deseeded and finely chopped

1 tbsp red wine vinegar

1 small red Romano pepper, deseeded and finely chopped

1 tbsp dried mint

2 sprigs of parsely

Cook the rice according to packet instructions. Drain and leave to cool under cold running water, then drain again. Preheat the grill.

Bring a large pan of water to the boil. Set up a large bowl of iced water nearby. Drop 4 razor clams into the boiling water, then fish them out almost immediately with a pair of tongs and drop them straight into the cold water. They should open but not cook. Repeat with the remaining clams.

Pull the clams out of their shells and prep them: use a pair of scissors to cut the black sack out of the clam, remove the 'beak', then chop the clams into thumbnail-sized pieces and put them into a bowl. Wash and dry 8 half-shells and set aside.

Put a tablespoon of oil into a large non-stick frying pan over a medium heat. Add the onion, garlic, tomatoes and chilli, and fry for about 15 minutes, or until the tomatoes and onions are soft but not brown. Blend (a hand blender in a small jug works well here) with the red wine vinegar to a smooth paste.

Wipe the frying pan and pour in a tablespoon of oil over a medium heat. Add the brown rice and fry for about 10 minutes, or until golden and crisp. Add the clams for the last couple of minutes.

Spread some of the sauce on the bottom of a half-shell, followed by some of the crispy rice and clams and Romano pepper pieces. Sprinkle with a little dried mint and parsley, and drizzle with olive oil. Repeat with the remaining half-shells.

Tip
See page 29.

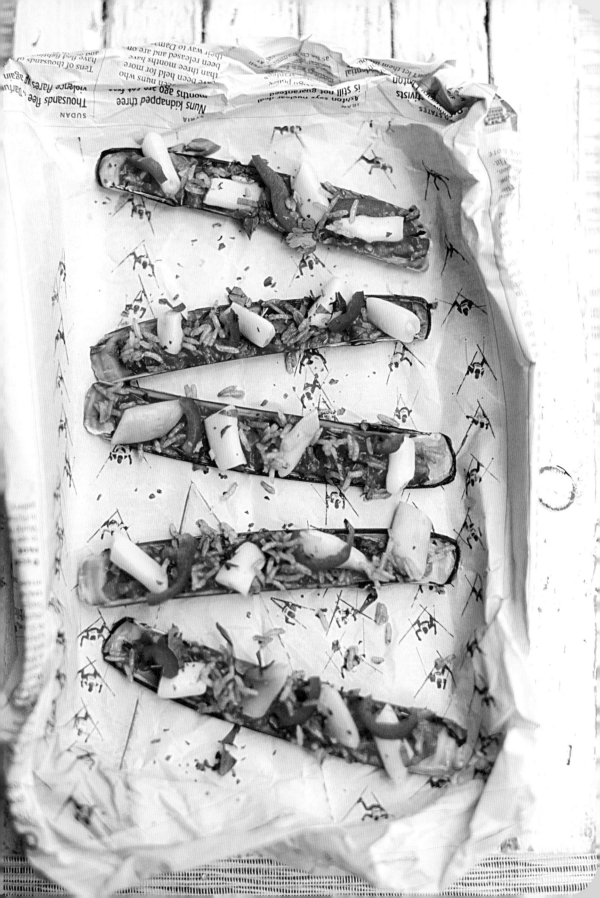

Little socca cakes with ratatouille

Serves	Preparation time:	Cooking time:
4 as a starter	20 minutes	1¼ hours

In Brittany they have crêpes and *galettes* (buckwheat pancakes), but in Nice they have *socca*. It's a sort of pancake made from chickpea flour, which is baked in a wood-fired oven and has a crispy, slightly blistered, charred crust. At home it's a little difficult to recreate that smoky flavour (unless you happen to have a wood-fired oven), but it's worth making nevertheless.

For the ratatouille

2 cloves of garlic, peeled and minced

1 onion, peeled and finely chopped

1 tsp fresh thyme leaves

3 tbsp olive oil

1 aubergine, thinly sliced

1 small courgette, thinly sliced

1 yellow pepper, thinly sliced

6 tomatoes, cut into quarters

a pinch of sugar

sea salt

For the anchovy sauce

10 anchovies (1 × 50g tin of anchovies in olive oil)

2 tbsp extra virgin olive oil or oil from the anchovy tin

zest and juice of ½ an unwaxed lemon

30ml water

For the socca

200g chickpea flour (also know as gram flour)

1 tsp dried oregano

1 tsp sea salt

3 tbsp olive oil for the batter, plus extra for frying

230ml water

Preheat the oven to 180°C (fan).

Gently fry the garlic, onion and thyme leaves in 2 tablespoons of oil. Once the onion is translucent and soft, add the aubergine and cook for around 5 minutes, or until soft.

Toss the remaining vegetables in a large roasting tin with a tablespoon of oil, the sugar and a little salt. Add the cooked onion and aubergine, and mix them together. Cover the tray with foil or baking paper, then bake for 1 hour.

In the meantime, make the sauce in a food processor by whizzing together the anchovies, oil, lemon zest and juice, and water. The sauce should be the consistency of double cream, so add a little more water if necessary. Set aside.

Now prepare the *socca*. Whisk the chickpea flour, oregano and salt with the oil and water. Put 1 teaspoon of oil into a non-stick frying pan over a medium-high heat, then ladle about 3 tablespoons of batter into a circle, creating an 8cm-diameter pancake. Cook for 1 minute on each side, or until golden. Repeat with the rest of the batter.

Divide the *socca* between the plates, then add a generous heap of ratatouille, followed by a drizzle of the anchovy sauce.

Tip
Be sure to get the pan nice and hot for the socca.

Get ahead
The socca can be made in advance, and kept wrapped in cling film. Reheat in the oven at 160°C (fan) for 20 minutes.

You can also make the ratatouille in advance and reheat it in the oven at 160°C (fan) for 20 minutes.

Burnt leek parcels with romesco sauce

Pass the parcel was one of my favourite party games as a kid. Who says you can't play it as a grown-up? This recipe is all about wrapping up some Catalonian flavours, letting your guests unpack the surprise.

Burning the leeks adds a slight smokiness, and for those who are a dab hand at burning things in the kitchen, this one is for you. The burnt parts are peeled off to reveal the juicy, sweet and tender leek underneath – perfect for dunking into the nutty, fresh romesco sauce. During springtime it's a Catalan tradition to serve romesco sauce with young spring onions, or *calçots*, which work in a similar way to leeks in this recipe.

3 medium red peppers

100g pine nuts

1 clove of garlic, peeled

4 tbsp extra virgin olive oil

20g fresh breadcrumbs

½ tsp sweet smoked paprika

1 tbsp sherry vinegar

optional: sea salt and lemon juice, to taste

12 medium leeks

Equipment

4 pages of newspaper

Preheat the grill to high. Cut your peppers in half and remove the seeds. Place skin side up on an oiled baking tray and grill for 15–20 minutes, or until black and tender. Then place in a plastic bag and leave to steam for about 20 minutes. When cool enough to handle, remove and discard the skins and set the flesh aside.

Toast the pine nuts in a small frying pan, shaking constantly for about 3 minutes, or until golden. Tip them on to a plate to cool. Place them in a blender or food processor with the grilled peppers, garlic, olive oil and breadcrumbs. Blitz and check the seasoning. Add the paprika for some heat, the sherry vinegar for an acidic kick, then salt and lemon juice if necessary.

Lay the leeks, spread apart, on a tray or rack (you may have to do this in batches). Grill for about 8 minutes, or until blackened, turning them every couple of minutes. Wrap 3 leeks in a piece of newspaper to make a parcel, then repeat with the remaining leeks so that you have 4 bundles. They will steam in the paper until ready to serve.

Place the romesco in a jar or bowl and let everyone open up their own parcel, peeling away the outer burnt leaves and dunking the soft, sweet interior straight into the sauce.

Tips
Try using Spanish Marcona almonds instead of pine nuts. These are often salted, so check the seasoning before adding any more salt to the sauce.

You can play around with the consistency of this sauce by altering the quantity of olive oil, and use it as a dressing or as a paste for crostini.

Get ahead
The romesco sauce will keep well in the fridge for 2–3 days.

Beetroot oatcakes with chicken liver parfait

Serves	Preparation time:	Cooking time:	Resting time:
4	40 minutes	40 minutes	2 hours minimum

This recipe is loosely inspired by the phenomenal 'meat fruit' at Heston Blumenthal's London restaurant, Dinner. The most perfectly glossy mandarin arrives at the table, which you cut open to reveal a silky chicken liver and foie gras parfait.

For the chicken liver parfait

50g salted butter

1 shallot, peeled and thinly sliced

2 cloves of garlic, peeled and crushed

2 sprigs of thyme

125g chicken livers, trimmed

1 tbsp brandy

½ tsp sea salt

¼ tsp finely ground pepper

For the jelly topping

1 gelatin leaf

75ml orange juice (juice of 1 orange)

1 tbsp sugar

1 small orange or clementine

For the oatcakes

50g raw beetroot (approx. ½ a beetroot)

30g oats

70g plain flour

½ tsp baking powder

½ tsp sea salt

½ tbsp sugar

50g butter, melted and cooled

Equipment

a 5cm cookie cutter

1 x 250ml clip top jar or ramekin

Melt a small knob of the salted butter in a large pan and add the shallot, garlic and thyme. Cook on a low heat for 5 minutes, or until the shallot has softened but hasn't browned. Turn up the heat and add the livers and brandy, then cook for about 2 minutes on each side, or until the livers have browned but are still slightly pink in the middle.

Leave to cool for 5 minutes. Remove the thyme, then whizz the livers in a food processor or blender with the remaining salted butter and the salt and pepper. Divide the parfait mixture between the small jars or ramekins and smooth the tops with a spoon. Leave in the fridge while you make the jelly.

Soak the gelatin leaf in cold water for 5–10 minutes. Pour the orange juice into a pan with the sugar. Heat until the sugar has dissolved. Squeeze the gelatin leaf and pour away the water. Strain the orange juice through a sieve directly on to the gelatin leaf. Stir to dissolve.

Peel the small orange or clementine with a paring knife, removing all the pith, and slice into thin rounds. Top the chicken liver parfait with an orange round, then pour the jelly mixture on top. Leave to set for at least 2 hours but preferably overnight.

To make the oatcakes, preheat the oven to 160°C (fan). Peel and finely grate the beetroot, then place in a bowl. Add the oats, plain flour, baking powder, salt and sugar, mix well, then add the cooled melted butter and bring together to form a ball.

Roll out with a rolling pin between two sheets of baking paper to about 4–5mm thick. Cut into rounds using a 5cm cookie cutter and put on a lined baking tray. Roll the leftover dough out again and cut out some more rounds, so that you have 16 oatcakes in total. Bake for 25–30 minutes, then leave to cool on a rack.

Get ahead

The parfait can be made 1–2 days before serving.

Poached fennel with pink prawns and toasted almonds

Serves
4

Preparation time:
10 minutes

Cooking time:
15 minutes

In my line of work I eat countless different dishes, and it's often pretty impossible to keep track of all those flavours. However, some memories stick with me. Grandma's cake, Mum's roast or a birthday dish are the easy ones to recall, but sometimes it can be the more unassuming dishes that make the biggest impact. The memory of eating fennel poached in milk at a friend's house in Milan many years ago is something that has stuck with me ever since. The lightly fragrant creamy broth with the tender fennel was divine. My recipe might have a few extras, but the hero is still the simple poached fennel.

1 large bulb of fennel (roughly 500g) or 2 small ones

200ml whole milk

100ml single cream

200ml hot vegetable stock

a pinch each of sea salt and white pepper

160g raw peeled king prawns, heads removed

30g flaked almonds

zest of 1 unwaxed lemon

extra virgin olive oil, to serve

Cut the fennel into quarters lengthways. Remove the fronds, setting them aside for later, then trim the toughest tips of the stalks and remove any scruffy outer leaves. Place the fennel quarters in a medium saucepan (the fennel should sit snugly), and pour in the milk, single cream, vegetable stock and salt and pepper.

Bring the pan to poaching point, cover and cook on a very low heat for 15 minutes, or until the fennel is tender, adding the prawns for the final 3–4 minutes of the cooking time. Take off the heat and check the seasoning. In the meantime, toast the almonds in a dry frying pan, tossing the pan until golden.

To serve, place a wedge of poached fennel in a shallow bowl and divide the prawns between the serving bowls. Pour over some of the hot broth, then sprinkle with toasted almonds and the fennel fronds. Scatter some lemon zest on top, and drizzle over a little oil.

Tips
Don't let the broth come to the boil or it might curdle.
You can use cooked prawns instead of raw; just add them for the final minute of cooking.

Get ahead
You can cook the fennel in advance and reheat it on a low heat, until warmed through. Raw fennel will discolour, however, if prepped ahead without cooking.

Hot butter and soy sauce mackerel with chopped salad

Serves	Preparation time:	Cooking time:
4 as a starter	15 minutes	5 minutes

Istanbul lies half in Europe and half in Asia and that fusion has influenced the local food greatly, just like the mix of Asian soy sauce and European butter that sit together happily in this dish.

Mackerel is everywhere in Istanbul, whether it's at the fish market, so fresh it's still flopping around, or being flipped over on a hot grill on a street food stand. It's cheap and very nutritious, rich in omega 3.

100g unsalted butter

For the salad

2 tbsp white wine vinegar

½ a red onion, peeled and thinly sliced

1 small Lebanese cucumber or ½ a regular cucumber, peeled

5 medium tomatoes, quartered

1 tbsp finely chopped fresh dill

a pinch of sea salt

1 tbsp pomegranate molasses

For the mackerel

2 tsp chopped fresh thyme leaves

1 tsp dried mint

4 mackerel fillets, deboned but skin left on

30ml light soy sauce or tamari

Equipment

a cheesecloth or muslin

Start by clarifying the butter. Heat it in a saucepan over a very low heat, until it's melted. Let it simmer gently until the foam rises to the top. Once the butter stops spluttering and no more foam seems to be rising to the surface, remove from the heat and skim off the foam with a spoon.

Line a mesh sieve with a cheesecloth or muslin and set the sieve over a bowl. Carefully pour the warm butter through the sieve into the bowl, leaving behind any solids from the bottom of the pan. Discard the milk solids left in the cheesecloth.

Meanwhile, put the white wine vinegar into a small bowl, add the red onion and leave to soak. Deseed the cucumber, cut into small cubes and put into a large bowl. Add the tomatoes and dill, sprinkle with the salt and mix together.

Mix together the thyme leaves and dried mint. Heat a large non-stick frying pan and put 1 tablespoon of the clarified butter into the pan. When the pan is smoking hot, add the mackerel fillets skin side down. Cook for 2 minutes before turning over and cooking for another 2 minutes.

Add the soy sauce to the remaining clarified butter. Drizzle the fish with the sauce and sprinkle with the herb mix. Toss the onion with the other salad ingredients and the pomegranate molasses.

Serve the mackerel on a bed of salad. Drizzle over a tablespoon of the cooking juices on to each mackerel fillet.

Tip
If you can't find pomegranate molasses, use a mixture of lemon juice and honey instead.

English garden salad

Serves
4

Preparation time:
45 minutes

Cooking time:
30 minutes

I love a salad, and I often wish salads got a little bit more attention as the highlight of a meal. They are all too often seen as diet food, carelessly pulled from a bag and tossed with a bottled dressing, but that's not how it's done in my home.

Making a great salad is all about being creative with your presentation. Don't just slice or chop; play around with dicing, making ribbons, batons . . . Different textures and temperatures are also key to a great salad. Crunchy, soft, creamy, hot and cold: don't be afraid to mix it up. I certainly haven't with my English garden salad.

1 tsp caster sugar

6 tbsp white wine vinegar

2 tbsp water

1 red onion, peeled and thinly sliced

2 medium potatoes, peeled and cut into 1cm cubes

8 rashers of smoked back bacon, finely chopped

1 small cucumber or ½ a regular cucumber

300g cottage cheese (see page 246, or shop-bought)

8 tbsp crème fraîche or Greek yoghurt

a small bunch of finely chopped chives

a pinch of sea salt

½ tsp freshly ground pepper

8 radishes, thinly sliced

2 handfuls of fresh peas

2 handfuls of salad leaves, washed

Dissolve the sugar in the vinegar and water in a small bowl. Add half the onion to the bowl and mix.

Place the cubes of potato in a medium saucepan. Cover with salted cold water, bring to the boil, then simmer for about 5 minutes, or until just tender. Drain.

Put the bacon into a large non-stick frying pan on a medium heat. Fry for 2 minutes, then add the other half of the onion and cook in the bacon fat for 10 minutes. Add the parboiled potatoes and cook for around 5–7 minutes, or until everything is lightly golden, stirring occasionally so everything browns evenly.

Meanwhile, peel ribbons from one half of the cucumber with a speed peeler. Cut the other half into small cubes.

Mix the cottage cheese with the crème fraîche, chives, salt and pepper. Taste and add more seasoning if desired. Drain the onion from the pickling liquid.

To assemble, spread the cottage cheese mixture on to four plates. Divide the hot potato and bacon mix between the plates, followed by the cubes and ribbons of cucumber, radish slices, fresh raw peas and salad leaves. Place some of the pickled onion on top, and serve immediately.

Haricot bean salad

Serves	Preparation time:	Soaking time:	Cooking time:
4 as a side	10 minutes	8 hours minimum	1-1½ hours

Dried pulses and legumes (e.g. chickpeas, lentils and haricot beans) seem to be among those items that are bought on a spur-of-the-moment health whim, but then lie forgotten at the back of the store cupboard for a couple of years.

Blow off the dust and make a delicious dish like this haricot bean salad. It's cheap and nutritious, and makes a surprisingly tasty alternative to bog-standard roast potatoes as a side dish for my Provençal roast chicken (see page 105).

200g dried haricot beans

2 tbsp red wine vinegar

3 tbsp extra virgin olive oil

a pinch each of sea salt and sugar

1 small red onion, peeled and finely chopped

a handful of chopped chives

freshly ground pepper

Soak the dried haricot beans in a large bowl of cold water overnight, or for about 8 hours. Drain the beans and place in a large saucepan with plenty of cold water to cover. Bring to the boil, skimming off any scum that comes to the surface, and cook for 1–1½ hours, topping up the water with just-boiled water if necessary. When the beans are tender, drain through a colander and set aside.

Make the dressing for the haricot salad. In a large bowl, whisk together the red wine vinegar with the oil, salt and sugar. Add the red onion and toss in the warm haricot beans.

Sprinkle with the chopped chives and pepper, and serve.

Tips

The salad can be made in advance and served at room temperature.

When seeing if the beans are cooked, check a few different ones as they can cook at different speeds.

If you don't have time to soak the beans, tinned beans are a good alternative. Rinse them well before using. However, when tossing them in the dressing, do so gently as they tend to be softer than the home-cooked variety. The equivalent quantity for this recipe is about 2 x 400g tins of cooked haricots (drained weight approx. 460g).

Roasted cauliflower and caraway salad

Serves	Preparation time:	Cooking time:
4 as a side or starter	10 minutes	25–30 minutes

Having spent my teenage years in Bavaria, I have had plenty of cabbage and caraway salads in my life as they're served at each and every beer festival. But cabbage isn't the only thing that goes particularly well with caraway: cauliflower works a treat too.

I small head of cauliflower (approx. 300g), trimmed and separated into bite-size florets

I tbsp olive oil

sea salt

2½ tbsp cider vinegar

½ tsp caster sugar

½ tsp English mustard

2 tsp caraway seeds

6 slices of smoked streaky bacon, finely chopped

I small red onion, peeled and finely sliced

I unpeeled apple, cored and sliced

a small handful of finely chopped fresh chives

Preheat the oven to 200°C (fan).

Toss the cauliflower florets in the oil and a pinch of salt, then roast in the oven for 20–25 minutes, or until golden.

In the meantime, whisk together the cider vinegar, sugar and mustard in a bowl. Dry-fry the caraway seeds in a frying pan until aromatic and add to the bowl, then return the pan to the heat.

Place the chopped bacon and onions in the pan and fry for around 5 minutes, or until the bacon is golden. Transfer to a salad bowl, then throw in the roasted cauliflower and diced apple, and mix. Pour over the dressing and toss everything together, then taste for salt and sprinkle over the chives. This dish can be served warm or cold.

Tips
You can use thinly sliced raw green cabbage instead of the cauliflower.
If you aren't a fan of caraway, try fennel seeds or cumin seeds instead.
You can leave the onion raw if you prefer. Finely slice it and add it to the vinaigrette to soak for a few minutes.

Get ahead
You can make this salad a day in advance, leave it in the fridge and serve at room temperature. You could also reheat it in the oven at 160°C (fan) for 15 minutes.

Panzanella

Serves
4

Preparation time:
40 minutes

Salting time:
30 minutes

Cooking time:
15 minutes

Stuffed with the sunny flavours of the Amalfi coast – roasted aubergines and tomatoes, dressed with a zingy caper and basil sauce – this is my take on the fantastic Italian bread salad. Panzanella is a great way to use up stale bread. When paired with tomatoes, it soaks up all the lovely juices and oil, giving it a new lease of life.

1 large round loaf of white sourdough bread (800g)

1 tbsp olive oil

500g heritage tomatoes, a mix of colours, quartered or halved if small

200g buffalo mozzarella, drained and torn

For the aubergines

2 small aubergines

3 tbsp sea salt

350ml water

150ml white wine vinegar

50g caster sugar

2 tbsp olive oil

For the basil and caper sauce

100ml extra virgin olive oil

2 tbsp lemon juice

1 small clove of garlic, peeled

20g fresh basil, leaves and stalks

1 tbsp capers, rinsed

sea salt

Trim the stems off the aubergines and cut them lengthways into 4mm-thick slices. Sprinkle generously with the salt and place in a colander in the sink for about 30 minutes. Rinse and pat dry with kitchen towel.

In the meantime, make the basil and caper sauce. In a food processor, blend together the oil, lemon juice, garlic, basil, capers and salt to taste, until you have a nice green sauce.

Place the water, vinegar and sugar in a large saucepan and bring to a simmer, allowing the sugar to dissolve. Blanch the aubergine slices in the liquid for 2 minutes or until just tender. Do this in 2 batches if necessary. Remove the aubergines with a slotted spoon and place in a colander to cool. Pat with paper towels to absorb any excess water.

Put a griddle pan on a high heat, and brush both sides of the aubergine slices with oil. When the griddle pan is smoking hot, sear the aubergine slices in batches for about 1 minute on each side, and set aside.

Trim the top off the loaf using a bread knife. Set the 'lid' aside and scoop out the insides of the bread, right to the crust. Tear the insides up into bite-sized pieces, and set half of them aside to use at a later date (they freeze well).

Heat 1 tablespoon of oil in a frying pan and, when hot, add the torn-up bread and fry for 2–3 minutes, or until golden brown. Place in a bowl with the tomatoes and toss together with the basil and caper sauce.

Arrange a generous layer of aubergines on the base of the bread. Add a layer of roughly torn mozzarella, then one of tomatoes and bread, and continue to layer the ingredients, making sure to press them into the bread bowl firmly to fit in as many as possible.

Place the lid on the bread bowl, wrap it tightly in cling film and set aside until serving. Remove the film and cut into thick slices.

Tip
Marinate any leftover aubergine in olive oil, salt, chopped chilli, garlic and parsley. Leave fully submerged in a sterilized jar in the fridge and it should keep for a week.

Get ahead
You can make this the day before and chill it overnight, tightly wrapped in cling film.

Chilled cucumber soup

Serves 4
(makes 700ml soup)

Preparation time:
15 minutes

Resting time:
15 minutes minimum

Inspiration for a recipe can come to me anywhere and this one, rather bizarrely, was inspired by a skiing trip to St Moritz. The land of rich and heavy fondues is the least likely place you would associate with a summery chilled cucumber soup. I, however, had the most amazing gin and tonic in the après-ski hours. The barman asked me whether I would like to have some pepper in it – a first for me. That hit of pepper with the juniper flavours of the gin and slice of cucumber was a revelation. I wanted to replicate that flavour combination in a dish, and came up with this vibrant and refreshing soup.

10 juniper berries

sea salt

2 large cucumbers (approx. 1kg total weight)

4 sticks of celery (you can leave the leaves on)

1–2 tbsp white wine vinegar, to taste

4 tbsp crème fraîche

white pepper

Equipment

a spice grinder

a blender

a muslin cloth

a mandolin

Grind the juniper berries with 1 teaspoon of salt into a fine powder in a spice grinder or using a pestle and mortar. Set 200g of cucumber to one side, then roughly chop the rest along with the celery. Place the chopped cucumber and celery in a blender, along with the white wine vinegar, and blend until as smooth as possible – in batches if necessary.

Line a sieve with muslin and place over a medium bowl. Pour the blended celery and cucumber through the muslin – again, in batches if necessary. Gather the corners of the muslin and twist so that all the juice is squeezed out. Pour the juice in a jug and place in the fridge for at least 30 minutes, or the freezer for 15 minutes. You want it to be ice-cold.

Transfer the pulp to a bowl and mix with the crème fraîche and the ground juniper berries. Taste for salt, then put into the fridge until needed.

Thinly slice the remaining 200g of cucumber with a mandolin to about 3mm thick, and season with salt and plenty of white pepper.

To serve, divide the cucumber broth between your bowls. Drain any liquid from the sliced cucumbers, then divide between the bowls. Place a heaped scoop of the crème fraîche and cucumber mixture on one tablespoon and use another to shape it into a neat rounded tablespoon shape (or quenelle). Add a quenelle to each bowl, and serve immediately.

Tips

The soup is lovely and simple on its own, but it also works well with ribbons of Parma or Serrano ham, cooked and shelled prawns, crayfish tails or some cooked crabmeat.

Keep your cucumber and celery in the fridge before making the soup: it will help it to chill more quickly.

SUN'S OUT IN STOCKHOLM

LOVE THE TYPOGRAPHY ON THIS BUTCHER'S SIGN

OLD TOWN IN WARSAW

RADIS 'GLAÇONS' - ICE RADISHES AT THE MARKET IN PARIS

ON THE PLANE AGAIN FOR ANOTHER ADVENTURE.

CAFÉS IN KARAKÖY, ISTANBUL

FISH DOESN'T GET FRESHER THAN IN MARSEILLE.

MY KIND OF BREAKFAST: OYSTERS AND PINK PRAWNS IN BORDEAUX

JUICE SHOP IN ISTANBUL

oregano

lavender

wild thyme

STOCKHOLM - VENICE OF THE NORTH

Smörgåstårta

The Swedes might not be known for their extravagant design, opting more for snow-white interiors and simple lines, but when it comes to the humble sandwich, they certainly know how to push the boat out. *Smörgåstårta* is a sandwich layer cake, filled with pâté, smoked fish, prawns, ham, cream cheese . . . basically, anything. They can be found in bakeries, supermarkets and even at the petrol station, and are served at parties, weddings, funerals and other social gatherings.

I went with the less-is-more approach for my filling, sticking with some key Swedish flavours: pickled beetroot, dill, quick-brined salmon and horseradish.

4 slices of Swedish flatbread (*polarbröd*) or a good-quality sliced white bread, crusts removed

For the quick-cured juniper salmon

250ml water

35g coarse salt

35g granulated sugar

1 tsp juniper berries

1 small raw beetroot

150g very fresh salmon fillet, skinned

For the horseradish cream

100ml whipping cream

1 tbsp horseradish cream

To decorate

1 small cucumber

1 small pickled beetroot

1 unwaxed lemon

a few sprigs of dill

2 tbsp salmon roe

Equipment

a speed peeler

a melon baller

a mandolin

For the salmon brine, put the water into a pan, along with the salt, sugar and juniper berries. Peel and roughly chop the raw beetroot and add it to the pan. Bring to the boil, simmer to dissolve the sugar and salt, leave to cool until it reaches room temperature, then place in the fridge to chill.

Finely slice the salmon into thin slivers. Drop into the cold brine for 7 minutes, then remove, drain and pat dry with kitchen towel. Discard the brine.

Whisk the whipping cream to firm-ish peaks, then fold in the horseradish cream.

Thinly spread each slice of bread with some of the cream and add a layer of salmon, then place the slices of bread on top of each other.

Take a speed peeler and peel thin ribbons from one side of the cucumber. Discard the first ribbon and don't use the seeded part: you need 4 perfect ribbons to wrap around the cake. With a melon baller, make enough to go around the edge of the bread from the other sides of the cucumber, discarding the middle seeded part.

Spread the rest of the cream around the outside edges and top of the bread (like icing a cake), making sure the cream is nice and smooth with a palette knife. Delicately place the cucumber ribbons around the edges of the sandwich cake.

Use a mandolin to make thin rounds of the pickled beetroot and very fine slices of the lemon. You can now decorate the top of your sandwich cake. I like to put cucumber balls around the top edge of the cake, then twist the remaining pieces of salmon around one finger to make a rose shape. Place these all over the top of the cake, along with slices of the pickled beetroot, the lemon slivers and sprigs of dill. Dot the salmon roe around. Chill until ready to serve.

Beef short ribs with crunchy slaw

Slow roasted pork belly with sloe gin

Mains

maple mustard gammon

'. . . every time a child says, "I don't believe in fairies," there is a fairy somewhere that falls down dead,' Peter replies.

That's how I feel every time a journalist asks me what my favourite dish is. OK, maybe comparing an interview question to the death of fairies is a little dramatic, but I do want to sigh every time I'm asked this. How can you ask someone who loves food what their favourite dish is? It's like asking Carrie from *Sex and the City* what her favourite pair of shoes is: it's impossible to answer. What I fancy eating depends on a) what the weather is like; b) where I am; and c) the state of my fridge.

The recipes I've crammed into this chapter are the result of various different cravings or scenarios. On a hot summer's day, try my chicken summer salad (page 126). When you need a quick dinner but have hardly anything in the fridge, my courgette linguine, with three different sauces to pick from (page 136), is perfect. When you'd like to impress the in-laws, there's my venison steak with celeriac purée, pickled blackberries and carrot petals (page 112). If you're entertaining a bunch of mates, my seafood chilli with tortilla bowls (page 94). For a veggie, low-carb dinner, my stir-fried cauliflower rice (page 121). For a simple, everyday dinner for the family, my Provençal roast chicken with roasted fennel (page 105); or for a comforting TV dinner to kick back with, my peeping mushroom pasta (page 79).

Another question I'm often asked is what you should cook for a romantic meal. My answer: don't. Well, not on your first date, or your second, and possibly not even on your third. Nerves are not what you need when you're slaving over a meal and trying to look your best. Trust me: having worked in professional kitchens, I know. However, if you're beyond the initial awkward dating stage, then a) do your homework and ask your date what they do or don't like (I learnt this lesson the hard way after serving meat to a veggie); b) keep it simple; and c) don't serve too much food (as this will make you sleepy . . . you get my drift). A few dishes to help you with your romantic encounters: my speedy summer bolognese (page 135), my one-tray roast (page 76) or my mushroom stroganoff with spinach and wild rice (page 124).

Whatever your appetite, there's a recipe sure to satisfy it.

London loaf three ways

Serves
2 as a main course
or 4–6 as a starter

Preparation time:
20 minutes

Proving time:
15 minutes minimum

Cooking time:
25 minutes

The London loaf – what is it? For me it used to be a bog-standard white sandwich loaf. But with so many different national cuisines found across London, the true bread of the city is far less strict than the 'London bloomer'. From the sourdough loaves crafted under archways in east London, to the Turkish *lahmacun* of Dalston and the naans of Brick Lane, there is no one bread that represents the city, but more a melting pot of doughs, revealing the diversity of the London food scene.

Flatbreads are the speediest of breads to make at home, and benefit the most from being freshly made to order. Here are three great ways to transform this simple dough into three delicious pizzas.

For the basic dough (makes 6 flatbreads)

250g plain flour, plus extra for dusting

1 tsp baking powder

1 tsp sea salt

110ml warm water

60ml natural yoghurt

1 tbsp vegetable oil

For the mince topping (enough for 2 flatbreads)

100g fine beef mince

5 cherry tomatoes, chopped

3 sage leaves, finely chopped

½ a red onion, peeled and finely chopped

½ tsp sea salt

½ tsp white pepper

For the cheesy filling (enough for 2 flatbreads)

2 cloves of garlic, peeled

3 sprigs of lemon thyme

1 x 125g ball of buffalo mozzarella cheese

sea salt and freshly ground pepper

a handful of fresh rocket

Mix together the flour, baking powder and salt in a large bowl. Make a well in the centre and pour in the liquid ingredients. Combine until you have a slightly sticky mixture. Turn out and knead for a good 5 minutes until you have a smooth ball. Leave to rest for 15 minutes in a bowl covered with cling film or a clean damp tea towel. (It's even better made one day ahead.)

Meanwhile, prepare the mince topping. Mix together the topping ingredients and set aside until needed.

For the cheesy filling, thinly slice the garlic, pick the leaves from the sprigs of thyme and tear the mozzarella roughly. Mix the garlic, thyme leaves and mozzarella in a small bowl with some salt and pepper and set aside.

For the sweet topping, mix the mascarpone with the lemon zest and maple syrup or honey. Cut the peach in half, remove the stone and slice thinly. Set aside.

Divide the flatbread dough into 6 balls. Lightly dust the work surface and use a rolling pin to roll out the dough balls into circles 16cm in diameter and 4–5mm thick.

Put a large non-stick frying pan on a high heat (do two at a time if you have two pans). Preheat the grill.

Put the first dough round in the pan. Press half the mince mixture evenly on top and cook for 2 minutes, or until the base is golden and crisp. Place the flatbread under the grill for a further 2–3 minutes, or until the meat is cooked. Repeat with another dough round and the remaining mince topping.

For the cheese-stuffed flatbreads, put half the filling in the centre of a dough round, along with half the rocket, leaving a margin around

For the sweet topping
(enough for 2 flatbreads)

2 heaped tbsp mascarpone cheese

zest of 1 unwaxed lemon

1 tbsp maple syrup or runny honey

1 ripe peach or nectarine

the edge. Fold the dough over to make a half-moon shape and press the edges to seal tightly. Place in the hot pan. Cook for 2–3 minutes on each side, or until golden. Repeat with another dough round and the remaining cheese filling and rocket.

For the final sweet breads, cook each dough round on one side for 2 minutes, then flip it over and cook the other side for another 2 minutes. Remove from the pan and spread the flavoured mascarpone over one side, then arrange the fruit on top. Serve immediately.

Tips

After you have rolled out the dough, work quite quickly as it can dry out. Alternatively, cover with a loose layer of cling film.

Be sure to heat your pan well before placing the dough in the pan.

Get ahead

The dough can be made the day before, wrapped and chilled in the fridge.

STEP BACK IN TIME
AT THIS ART SHOP.

LOVE THE VIEW FROM THE
FRONT SEATS ON A
LONDON DOUBLE DECKER

CLASSIC PIE 'N' MASH SHOP,
EAST LONDON

CATCHING SOME SUN RAYS
ON A DALSTON ROOF TOP

RAINY SUNDAY ACTIVITY!
SORTING OUT PHOTOS!

DELICIOUS SMELLS WAFTING
AROUND BRIXTON MARKET

BRITISH RED POSTBOXES
ARE THE BEST!

A LITTLE BIT OF PINK
AND A FULL MOON

DON'T SEE MANY OF THESE
AROUND TOWN ANY MORE.

55 SHOREDITCH
LONDON

TELEPHONE

VICTORIA LINE

BLACKHORSE ROAD

WALTHAMSTOW CENTRAL

TOTTENHAM HALE

SEVEN SISTERS

FINSBURY PARK

EUSTON

HIGHBURY & ISLINGTON

KING'S CROSS-ST PANCRAS

WARREN STREET

OXFORD CIRCUS

GREEN PARK

VICTORIA

PIMLICO

VAUXHALL

STOCKWELL

BRIXTON

Underground

Potato crumpets with maple mustard gammon

Serves	Preparation time:	Resting time:	Cooking time:
4	30 minutes	1–2 hours	40 minutes

Back when I was a kid, breakfast for dinner was far more de rigueur, whether it was a sneaky fry-up, beans on toast, or kippers. This is a fancy version of a fry-up. Here the pillowy potato crumpets stand in for the more traditional heavy hash browns, while the blistered tomatoes are a speedy and fresh substitute for ketchup.

170ml milk

100–110ml water

160g potato flour

80g plain white flour

7g fast-action yeast

250g cherry tomatoes on the vine

sea salt

½ tsp baking powder

4–6 tbsp sunflower or vegetable oil

2 large gammon steaks (450g in total)

2 tsp English mustard

2 tsp maple syrup

4 eggs

Equipment

an 8cm cookie cutter

4 x 9cm pastry rings

Warm the milk and water gently in a small saucepan. Put the flours and yeast into a bowl and mix well. Add the milk and water and whisk until smooth. It will be the consistency of single cream. Cover with cling film and leave to rest at room temperature for 1–2 hours, or until bubbles have formed on the surface.

Preheat the oven to 200°C (fan). Put the tomatoes on a lined baking tray, sprinkle with salt and place in the oven for 10 minutes, or until they have burst. Set aside and turn the oven down to 160°C.

Whisk ½ teaspoon of salt and the baking powder into the crumpet batter. Put a heavy-based frying pan over a medium-high heat and pour in 2 tablespoons of oil. Oil a pastry ring, place it in the pan and pour 80ml of batter into it. Turn the heat down to medium-low and cook for 5 minutes or so, or until the surface has just set and bubbles have formed. Remove the ring and flip the crumpet over. Cook for 2–3 minutes, or until golden on the other side.

Repeat with the remaining batter; this should make 5 crumpets in total. Set aside on a wire rack.

Put another tablespoon of oil into a large frying pan and heat until medium-hot. Add the gammon steaks and cook for 1–2 minutes on one side. Flip them over and fry for 1 more minute. Spread the tops with the mustard, then the maple syrup, and slide out of the pan. Use the 8cm cookie cutter to cut out 4 pieces from the gammon steaks. Keep warm on a baking tray in the oven while you make the eggs.

Oil the pastry rings once again. Put a tablespoon of oil in the pan, crack the eggs into the rings, and fry the eggs for 2–3 minutes, or until the white has set. To serve, divide the potato crumpets between 4 plates. Put a gammon slice and fried egg on top of each one, and drape the vine tomatoes over them.

Bread-wrapped lamb kebabs

Serves
2–4

Preparation time:
20 minutes

Cooking time:
15 minutes

Istanbul really is the capital of street food, but not of the greasy fast-food variety. On every street corner you can spot people grilling fish, meat and vegetables; the smells waft through the air, luring you over.

A tasty mix of grilled meat wrapped in flatbread to soak up the flavoursome juices, some fresh grilled peppers and a soothing yoghurt and pomegranate sauce on the side is what a truly tasty Turkish kebab is about.

olive oil

1 iceberg lettuce, cut into wedges, to serve

For the super-speedy flatbread

170g strong bread flour, plus extra for dusting

1 tsp sea salt

100ml hot water

For the vegetable skewers (makes 4)

4 small green peppers (Turkish if possible), cut into 3 horizontally

3 red onions

For the lamb kebabs (makes 4)

100g mix of lamb kidneys and liver

200g minced lamb

½ tsp hot chilli flakes

1 tsp sea salt

½ tsp sumac

1 tbsp fresh thyme leaves

For the yoghurt dressing

150ml runny yoghurt

1 tbsp pomegranate molasses

sea salt and freshly ground pepper

Equipment

8 wooden skewers, soaked in water for 30 minutes

Put the flour and salt in a large bowl. Pour in the hot water and knead for 2–3 minutes, until you have a smooth ball of dough. Set aside, covered by a clean damp tea towel (don't skip this, as the dough will dry out), while you prepare the kebabs.

Peel and quarter the onions, keeping the stems intact, then thread the vegetables on to 4 skewers, alternating the colours.

Very finely chop the kidneys and liver. Mix together with the mince, hot chilli flakes, sea salt, sumac and thyme leaves, and massage together to combine. Divide the meat into 4 and squeeze it on to the end of each skewer, covering about 10cm. Set aside.

Preheat the grill to high. Divide the dough into 4 pieces. Roll each one out into a rectangle on a floured surface, as thinly as you can (use the size of the meat part of your kebab as a guide as you want it to wrap around the kebab, covering the meat).

Rub the lamb kebabs in a little oil. Grill for 1 minute on each side, then take off the heat. Wrap the flatbread around the skewer until the meat is just covered, then trim away the excess dough (you can discard this). Seal the overlap with a dab of water, squeeze the ends of the kebab together lightly, and place on a lined baking tray. Repeat with the remaining kebabs and rub them with oil. Place under the grill, turning regularly for around 7 minutes, or until the dough is golden and thoroughly cooked.

Rub the vegetable skewers with a little oil and heat a griddle pan or the grill of your oven. Cook for around 5 minutes, or until charred on each side.

Place the yoghurt in a bowl, swirl the pomegranate molasses through and season with salt and pepper. Serve with the lamb kebabs, vegetable skewers and wedges of iceberg.

Swiss chard is a common fixture on menus in the Nice region. But, oddly, it's more popular in pastry shops and bakeries than anywhere else, where it fills the famous tourte de blette, a sweet pastry that is also filled with raisins, pine nuts and sometimes pastry cream. It's quite an acquired taste, to say the least. I even spotted chard ice cream in Nice's most famous ice-cream parlour, Fenocchio, which offers some other unusual flavours too, such as black olive and sun-dried tomato.

Confit cod with rainbow chard gratin

Serves	Preparation time:	Cooking time:
4	20 minutes	30 minutes

sea salt and freshly ground pepper

For the chard gratin

250g rainbow chard, stalks cut into 3cm pieces and leaves cut into wide ribbons

250g crème fraîche

2 egg yolks

100g Parmesan cheese, finely grated

2 tbsp olive oil

2 large slices of sourdough bread, torn into large 'crumbs'

For the cod

4 cloves of garlic

750ml olive oil

zest of 1 unwaxed lemon

4 sprigs of thyme

4 x 150g cod fillets (thick, middle piece of cod), skinned and deboned; remove from fridge 30 minutes before cooking

For the persillade

2 cloves of garlic, peeled and minced

a small handful of finely chopped fresh flat-leaf parsley leaves

3 tbsp extra virgin olive oil

2 tsp white wine vinegar

Equipment

an ovenproof dish, approx. 19cm x 21cm

While northern France is all about butter, head down south to Provence and olive oil is everywhere. Traditionally, to 'confit' means to cook duck legs or other meat slowly in their own fat. My version makes the most of the local olive oil and is lightened with the use of white fish; the slow poaching keeps its delicate texture.

Bring a large saucepan of water to the boil, add the chard stalks and blanch for 5 minutes, adding the leaves for the final 2 minutes. Drain and cool in running water before leaving to drain thoroughly.

In a bowl, mix the crème fraîche with the egg yolks and half the Parmesan cheese, then season with salt and pepper.

Place the drained chard in your ovenproof dish. Pour the crème fraîche mixture over the top. Sprinkle with the remaining cheese and bake for 20 minutes at 180°C (fan).

Peel the garlic and put in a large sauté pan with the oil. Add the lemon zest, along with the thyme sprigs. Gently heat the oil until bubbles are coming off the garlic, but it isn't cooking quickly. You want it to have small bubbles but no sizzle.

Place the cod fillets in the pan and keep on the lowest heat, cooking them for 5–8 minutes, depending on the thickness of the cod. You will notice the texture change and the colour turn opaque when ready.

Meanwhile, make the croutons for the gratin. Heat the oil in a frying pan, then stir in the bread. Cook the croutons for about 4 minutes, stirring often, until a nice deep golden brown.

Mix together the ingredients for the persillade in a small bowl, then season with salt and pepper. Remove the chard gratin from the oven and sprinkle over the crispy croutons.

Drain the cod from the oil and season while warm. Serve with the chard gratin, and a spoonful of persillade on top.

One—tray roast

Serves
4

Preparation time:
20 minutes

Cooking time:
1 hour 40 minutes

My interest in roasting quails stemmed from the limitations of my *Little Paris Kitchen* oven. Chickens and turkeys are tricky to cook at the best of times, even in large kitchens. Ideally they are brined the day before, roasted while all the vegetables are also in the oven, and presented on an impressive plate at the table. But my little Paris kitchen was no place for such endeavours. So I learnt to adapt a traditional roast for pocket-sized feasts. Quails are dinky and delicious, and fit snugly on a small roasting tray, the only kind that would fit in my shoebox-sized oven.

4 medium-sized oven-ready quails (600g in total)

sea salt and freshly ground pepper

1 unwaxed lemon

1 x 330ml bottle of light-coloured beer

100g runny honey

20g fresh flat-leaf parsley

4 pork sausages (280g in total)

8 carrots, peeled and halved lengthways

350g new potatoes, washed and halved

1 heaped tbsp wholegrain mustard

100ml single cream

Equipment

butcher's string, to truss

Preheat the oven to 200°C (fan).

Season the quails with plenty of salt and pepper. Zest the lemon and rub into the skin with the seasoning.

Juice the lemon, keeping the skins. Mix the beer with the honey and lemon juice, and set aside.

Finely chop the parsley and the remaining juiced lemon skins, removing the pips. Remove and discard the casing from the sausages and mix the sausage meat with the parsley, lemon and some salt and pepper.

Stuff the quail cavities with the sausage-meat mix. There is a generous amount and it needs to be pushed in to fit. Take 4 long pieces of string and truss each quail around the legs to enclose the filled cavity. Place the quails breast side down in a roasting tin with the carrots and potatoes.

Pour over the beer marinade and cover with foil. Roast for 1 hour before removing the foil and turning each quail over, so that they're breast side up. Roast uncovered for another 25 minutes, or until the quail are golden and the juices run clear when the meat is poked with a sharp knife.

Drain all the roasting tin juices into a large frying pan. Set the quail and vegetables aside, covered with foil. Bring the cooking juices to a boil and cook for about 7–8 minutes, or until reduced by half. Stir in the mustard and cream, and taste for seasoning.

Pour the creamy sauce over the quail, carrots and potatoes, and serve immediately.

Tip
The pork sausage can be substituted with other minced meat.

Peeping mushroom pasta

Serves
4

Preparation time:
30 minutes

Cooking time:
40 minutes

Creamy sauce and earthy mushrooms is a tried and tested combination that never fails. Many might think it's a little boring and old school, but I've discovered a fun way of pepping up an old classic. Replace boring button mushrooms with some exotic Asian mushrooms and the recipe gets an instant facelift; pair them with lots of bubbling cheese and you are on to a winner.

30g butter

30g plain flour

500ml lukewarm milk

¼ of an onion, peeled

1 clove

1 bay leaf

250g rigatoni pasta

a pinch of freshly ground nutmeg

sea salt and white pepper

2 tbsp grainy mustard

100g Gruyère, Parmesan or other mature hard cheese, grated

170g mixed exotic mushrooms (e.g. shimeji, enoki), trimmed and torn into single mushrooms

finely chopped fresh parsley, to serve

Equipment

4 round baking dishes, approx. 10cm in diameter and 6cm deep

To make the béchamel sauce, melt the butter in a large pan over a medium heat. Add the flour and beat hard to form a paste, cooking it for 2 minutes. Take off the heat and leave to cool for 2 minutes, then gradually add the milk, whisking constantly.

Place the pan back over a medium heat, add the onion, clove and bay leaf, and simmer gently for 10 minutes, whisking frequently. If the sauce becomes too thick, whisk in a little more milk. While the sauce is simmering, preheat the oven to 180°C (fan).

Put the pasta in boiling salted water and cook for 2 minutes less than the packet instructions say. Finish the sauce by removing the onion, clove and bay leaf, then adding the nutmeg and seasoning with salt and white pepper (although black pepper is fine if you don't mind the speckles). Stir in the mustard and 40g of the cheese.

Drain the pasta and arrange the rigatoni pieces upright tightly in your 4 ovenproof dishes; they will look a bit like honeycomb. Pour the sauce over the pasta. Tap the base of the baking dishes to allow the sauce to get between the holes, spooning more on if necessary. Place the mushroom stalks into the rigatoni holes, leaving the caps poking out. Sprinkle with the remaining cheese and place in the oven.

Bake for 20–25 minutes, or until the cheese is golden and bubbling. Serve with a sprinkle of finely chopped parsley on top.

Get ahead

Make up the pasta dishes a few hours before, but add 10 minutes to the cooking time if baking from chilled.

The béchamel sauce can be made up to one day in advance. Place some cling film directly on the sauce if storing in the fridge, otherwise a skin will form. Whisk well to break up any lumps before using.

Salt beef with horseradish mash

Serves	Preparation time:	Curing time:	Cooking time:
4–6	45 minutes	3–10 days	3–4 hours

1kg piece of beef brisket

1 onion

1 carrot

1 stick of celery

1 bay leaf

5 black peppercorns

cornichons or sliced gherkins, to serve

For the brine

100g light brown muscovado sugar

150g coarse sea salt

1 tsp black peppercorns

4 juniper berries, lightly bruised

2 star anise

4 cloves

3 bay leaves

1.5 litres water

For the dill vinaigrette

10g fresh dill

4 tbsp sunflower oil

4 tbsp white wine vinegar

1 tsp sea salt

a large pinch of caster sugar

For the mash

1kg floury potatoes (e.g. Maris Piper or King Edward)

2 knobs of butter

100–200ml milk, warmed

1 tbsp horseradish cream

sea salt

Brisket is a fatty and great-value cut from the front underside of the cow. It is most commonly used to make pastrami and salt beef, which has seen quite a comeback in recent years. For many, however, it has always been on the map, particularly for fans like myself who make a regular pilgrimage to Beigel Bake on Brick Lane for their exemplary salt beef bagels with lashings of English mustard.

Place the ingredients for the brine in a large saucepan. Bring to the boil and simmer for 5 minutes, stirring to dissolve the salt and sugar. Leave to cool completely.

Place your beef in a plastic lidded container and pour the brine over the top. Make sure it is fully submerged (you may have to weight it down with something) and place in the fridge for a minimum of 3 days and up to 10 days. Turn the meat daily.

When ready to cook, drain the beef, discarding the marinade, and rinse under cold running water. Place in a large saucepan and cover with 3 litres of cold water. Peel and halve the onion, carrot and celery and add to the pan, along with the bay leaf and peppercorns. Gently bring to a simmer, skimming off any scum that comes to the surface. Poach really gently, uncovered, for 3–4 hours, topping it up with just-boiled water if necessary.

Make the dill vinaigrette by whizzing the dill (stalks included) in a food processor or blender with the other ingredients. Taste and add more salt if desired.

Peel the potatoes and boil them in salted water for 20–25 minutes, or until tender. Drain and put back into the pan over a medium heat, stirring constantly, until dry. Once the potatoes have stopped steaming, mash them (a potato ricer or Mouli gives the best results). Mix with the butter and add enough warm milk to make a smooth, creamy mash. Add the horseradish cream and a little salt.

When the salt beef is ready, remove it from the pan and place on a board, then slice it up thinly. Serve the salt beef, warm or hot, with the mash on the side and plenty of cornichons or sliced gherkins. Drizzle over the dill vinaigrette.

Get ahead
The beef freezes well once cooked. The vinaigrette can be made a day in advance.

Slow-roasted pork belly with sloe gin

Serves	Preparation time:	Marinating time:	Cooking time:
4–6	30 minutes	4 hours or overnight	3½–4 hours

Slow-cooked pork belly has to be one of the most tender cuts, thanks to the rich layers of fat that sandwich the flesh. I like to offset the fattiness of the meat with something fresh and crunchy, which is where the iceberg wedge comes into play. Try this dish as a lighter and more summery take on the traditional roast belly of pork.

1kg piece boneless pork belly, skin scored and patted dry

1 tbsp sea salt flakes

4 red onions

1 head of iceberg lettuce

1 unwaxed lemon

200g thick Greek yoghurt

a pinch each of sugar and sea salt

For the marinade

150ml sloe gin

80g runny honey

2 tsp white pepper

1 tbsp red wine vinegar

200g redcurrants or mixed berries (frozen is fine), plus a handful to garnish

Mix the marinade ingredients in a shallow glass or ceramic dish. Place the pork in it carefully, making sure that the marinade doesn't touch the skin. Leave uncovered and place in the fridge for 4 hours or overnight.

When the marinating time is up, preheat the oven to 220°C (fan). Pat the skin of the pork dry with kitchen towel. Place on a tray, setting the marinade to one side, and use a blow-dryer for 2–3 minutes to remove all the excess moisture from the skin. Rub the skin thoroughly with salt flakes, getting into the scoring.

Peel the red onions, cut into quarters and place at the bottom of a roasting tin, then pour over the marinade and lay the pork belly skin side up on top. Roast for 30 minutes, then turn the heat down to 150°C and roast for 2½–3 hours, or until very tender.

Remove the pork from the oven. Take the onions out and set aside. Crank up the heat again to 220°C and place the pork back in the oven for about 10 minutes, or until the skin is crispy.

Remove the pork from the oven. When cool enough to handle, separate the skin from the flesh. Slice the pork belly into slivers and chop the skin into small crouton-sized pieces. Cut the lettuce into thick slices, then wash and dry (keeping them whole).

Finely zest the lemon and mix into the Greek yoghurt with the sugar and salt. Add a squeeze of lemon juice.

To serve, place a large wedge of iceberg on a plate and top with the pork, onions, skin and berries. Drizzle with the yoghurt dressing.

Tip
If you can't get hold of sloe gin, use cassis or a light fruity red wine like Grenache.

Get ahead
Marinate the pork belly up to 2 days in advance.

Seafood paella nests

Serves	Preparation time:	Cooking time:
6	25 minutes	1 hour

The traditional rice-based paella has travelled far beyond its Valencian birthplace; I see giant paella pans bubbling away at my local market on a Saturday. But when I visited Toc al Mar, a quiet nook along the Spanish coast, I discovered a delicious, little-known variation known as *fiduea*, made with vermicelli noodles. Inspired by this discovery, I decided to make my own version, but my paella nests are too tantalizing a secret not to share.

2 tbsp olive oil

1 medium onion, peeled, halved and finely sliced

1 small bulb of fennel, trimmed and finely sliced

2 cloves of garlic, peeled and sliced

1 chorizo cooking sausage, cut into thin rounds

150ml dry white wine

a generous pinch of saffron

750ml fish stock

250g unshelled raw king prawns

200g cod or monkfish cheeks

150g purple sprouting broccoli, roughly chopped, tough stalks discarded

600g mixture of clams and mussels, cleaned

For the vermicelli nests

140g rice vermicelli noodles

2 knobs of soft butter

Equipment

a 6-hole muffin tin

Preheat your oven to 200°C (fan). Put the oil into a large lidded pan and sweat the onion, fennel and garlic over a low heat for 10 minutes.

Put the noodles in a bowl, pour boiling water over them, then leave for about 20 seconds, or until they are pliable but still have bite. Drain and spread out on a clean tea towel to get rid of excess moisture. Pat dry with another tea towel until they are really dry. Brush the muffin holes with the butter and line the holes with the noodles. Make sure you push the noodles right to the top of the muffin holes, as they will shrink slightly. Place in the oven for 20–25 minutes, or until crisp and golden.

Add the chorizo to the onion mixture and fry uncovered for 8–10 minutes, or until golden. Add the white wine and saffron, and simmer for a minute before adding the stock. Bring to the boil. Add the prawns, fish cheeks and broccoli stalks to the pan, and stir through. Simmer for 1 minute, then add the clams, mussels and broccoli tops. Toss through the sauce, cover with the lid, crank up the heat and cook for 3 minutes.

Strain the stew through a colander over a large bowl. Return the liquid to the pan and simmer for about 20 minutes, or until reduced to your desired consistency (either a broth or a rich sauce).

Meanwhile, remove some of the mussels and clams from their shells and return to the fish and broccoli mixture, then cover with aluminium foil to keep warm.

Remove the vermicelli nests from the oven and divide between large shallow bowls. Add a ladle full of the seafood to each of the nests, then pour the sauce over the top. Arrange the fish and broccoli around the edge of the nests.

Get ahead

The nests can be made in advance and kept in an airtight container for a day or two.

Spice—rubbed trout with giant couscous and green beans

Serves
4

Preparation time:
30 minutes

Cooking time:
20 minutes

When it comes to spice rubs, I have some friends who guard their personal recipe the same way Coca-Cola guard theirs. I, however, am happy to share my special blend of spices. Making your own custom spice rub is probably the simplest way of adding your own personal touch to dishes. This recipe is really just a starting point and can be easily adapted to your taste. Once you get the hang of balancing the flavours, the possibilities are endless.

4 whole trout (approx. 300g each), gutted and scaled

1½ unwaxed lemons

1 small bulb of fennel (250g), halved and finely sliced, keeping the leafy tops

a large handful of roughly chopped fresh flat-leaf parsley leaves

200g giant couscous

250g French green beans, trimmed and cut into 1cm rounds

1 tbsp olive oil

sea salt

For the spice rub

2 tbsp sumac

1 tbsp smoked paprika

1 tbsp sugar

1 tbsp sea salt

1 tbsp ground cumin

½ tbsp ground ginger

½ tbsp ground cinnamon

Preheat the grill to high. Blend the ingredients for the spice rub in a pestle and mortar.

Smear the spice rub generously all over the outside and inside of the trout, then place on a foil-lined, lightly oiled baking tray.

Thinly slice one of the lemons. Stuff the fennel, parsley and lemon slices inside the cavity of the fish. Place the fish under the grill. Grill for 5–10 minutes on one side, then turn the fish over and cook for a further 5 minutes on the other.

Meanwhile, bring a pot of salted water to the boil and add the giant couscous. Boil for 3 minutes, then add the French green beans. Cook for a further 2 minutes, or until al dente, and drain.

Zest and juice the remaining ½ a lemon. Toss the beans with the oil, lemon zest and juice and a little salt. Serve each fish whole with the couscous on the side. Garnish with the leafy fennel tops.

Tip
This spice rub works well with all sorts of other things. Try spreading it on aubergine slices and drizzling with a little oil before grilling. It's also a great rub for chicken.

Get ahead
Make the spice rub a few days before and keep in a sealed jar. You can easily double the quantity and store it to season other dishes.

Beef short ribs with crunchy slaw

Serves	Preparation time:	Marinating time:	Cooking time:
4	20 minutes	1 hour–2 days	2½–3½ hours

I have a fond memory of my Austrian grandma eating ribs with a big bib stuck into the collar of her dress. I think the best way of eating ribs is with your fingers. This is definitely finger food – not in the dainty, ladylike sense, but more in the messy, get-stuck-right-in kind of way.

1.5–2kg beef short ribs (Jacob's ladder)

2 spring onions, finely chopped, to garnish

For the marinade

1 x 400g tin of cherry tomatoes, chopped

50g dark brown sugar

1 tbsp tomato purée

1 dried chipotle chilli, finely chopped

2 tsp white pepper

100ml red wine vinegar

1 tbsp fish or Worcestershire sauce

5 cloves of garlic, peeled and minced

For the slaw

250g celeriac

1 crunchy red dessert apple

4 carrots

150g crème fraîche

4 tbsp white wine vinegar

1 tbsp wholegrain mustard

a pinch of caster sugar

sea salt and freshly ground pepper

Put all the marinade ingredients into a bowl and mix well. Place the ribs with the marinade in a large bag to marinate for at least an hour (best several hours or overnight).

Preheat the oven to 150°C (fan). Remove the ribs and the marinade from the bag and put into a large tray. Cover with aluminium foil and roast for 2–3 hours, or until the meat is tender and beginning to fall apart.

Increase the oven temperature to 200°C (fan). Remove the foil and baste the ribs with the marinade. Roast for a further 30 minutes, basting another couple of times.

The sauce should be sticky and thick and the ribs dark and glossy. Remove from the oven and leave to cool until you can pick them up with your fingers. If you want to thicken the sauce further, remove the ribs, cover them in foil and set aside. Place the sauce in a small saucepan and simmer until it's the desired consistency, then brush over the ribs before serving.

In the meantime, make the coleslaw. Peel, then cut the celeriac and carrots into fine little matchsticks, or grate them. A mandolin or food processor works well for this. Peel and core the apple, then cut into matchsticks or grate. Put all the salad ingredients into a bowl. Whisk together the rest of the slaw ingredients and toss through the salad. Taste for seasoning.

Line the ribs up and sprinkle with spring onions down the middle. Serve with the salad on the side.

Tip
Using a mandolin to julienne your vegetables really makes a difference. The slaw will have a crunchier texture (grating it will make the slaw wetter).

Get ahead
You can marinate the ribs up to 2 days in advance.
Make sure you prepare the salad at the last moment; the celeriac and apple will go brown otherwise.

Pasta pizza bianca e rossa

Serves	Preparation time:	Cooking time:
4–6	15 minutes	30 minutes

I nipped into quite a few bakeries while visiting Naples, and kept spotting deep-fried pasta balls, stuffed with peas, pork mince and béchamel sauce, known as *frittatine di pasta;* apparently the recipe was born from using up leftover pasta. I love recipes that don't let anything go to waste, and that's where the pasta pizza came from. When you can't decide whether you want a slice of pizza or a bowl of pasta, have a pasta pizza.

300g dried spaghetti (makes 2 pizza bases)

2 tbsp olive oil, plus extra to drizzle

4 eggs

a pinch of dried oregano

½ tsp sea salt

½ tsp freshly ground pepper

For the *rossa*

1 x 400g tin of cherry tomatoes

1 tsp dried oregano

a good pinch of sugar

a pinch of sea salt

50g black olives, drained and pitted

6 anchovy fillets, drained

6 large fresh basil leaves

For the *bianca*

125g soft goat's cheese

6 slices of Parma ham

optional: ½ teaspoon chilli flakes

Equipment

an ovenproof non-stick frying pan, approx. 25cm diameter

Cook the spaghetti in boiling salted water for around 10 minutes, or until al dente, then drain.

Preheat the grill to high. In the meantime, start to make the *rossa* sauce. Put the tinned tomatoes and oregano into a medium-sized saucepan with the sugar and salt and bring to a simmer. Cook for 5 minutes, then blend with a hand blender until smooth, seasoning again if necessary.

Tip the pasta on to a clean tea towel and roll the pasta in it to remove all excess moisture. In a large bowl, beat the eggs with the oregano, salt and pepper. Place the pasta in the bowl with the eggs and toss to coat thoroughly. This is easier to do with your hands.

Put a large ovenproof frying pan on a medium heat and pour in 1 tablespoon of oil. When the oil in the frying pan is really hot, add half the pasta and spread out evenly across the surface of the pan. Fry for 4 minutes, or until the base is really golden and crunchy.

Scatter the goat's cheese in even lumps over the top. Place under the grill for 4–5 minutes. Tear over the Parma ham in ribbons, then drizzle with a little olive oil and add the chilli flakes (if using).

Fry the remaining pasta to make a second pasta pizza base. When cooked, put the tomato sauce on top, along with the olives and anchovies. Place under the grill for 4–5 minutes as before, then scatter with the basil leaves.

Tips

This is a great way of using up leftover pasta; you need around 550–600g cooked weight of spaghetti.

Make sure the oil is nice and hot before the pasta goes in the pan.

Don't skip the drying stage of the pasta preparation or you will end up with a watery mixture.

Ham hock lunchbox

Serves
4–6 for a picnic

Preparation time:
20 minutes

Cooking time:
3½–4½ hours

I was the queen of packed lunches when I had an office job in London. My boss would often make fun of me, saying my packed lunch resembled a three-course meal. I certainly wasn't content with a soggy sandwich from the local garage. Now I work mainly from home, a lunchbox isn't so important; however, I do like to head out to the park when the sun is shining, and this is a perfect portable lunch.

2 lightly smoked ham hocks (about 1.2kg each)

2 onions, peeled and halved

2 carrots, peeled and halved lengthways

2 sticks of celery, halved

2 bay leaves

1 tsp whole black peppercorns

250g sugar snap peas

2 tbsp olive oil

1 tbsp balsamic vinegar

sea salt and freshly ground pepper

For the potato salad

500g Jersey Royals or baby new potatoes, scrubbed

125g crème fraîche

3 tbsp chopped chives

juice of ½ a lemon

Place the ham hocks in a large saucepan and cover with cold water, then bring to the boil. Boil for 2–3 minutes, then drain. Return the ham hocks to the pan and cover once more with cold water. Add the onions, carrots, celery, bay leaves and whole peppercorns.

Bring to the boil over a medium heat, skimming off any scum that rises to the surface. Turn down the heat and simmer uncovered for 3–4 hours, or until the flesh from the ham hock is tender enough to pull away from the bone. Top up with just-boiled water if necessary. Drain the liquid (keep this, as it makes a great stock for the speedy one-pot noodle on page 102) and leave the hocks to cool.

Place the potatoes in a pan of cold salted water, bring to the boil and cook for around 15–20 minutes, or until tender.

Mix the crème fraîche, chives and lemon juice in a small bowl, then season with salt and pepper to taste. Drain the potatoes well in a large colander and crush gently with the back of a fork (breaking them up allows the dressing to penetrate better). Transfer the potatoes to a large bowl and fold through the crème fraîche dressing while they're still warm, then leave to cool completely.

Cook the sugar snap peas in boiling salted water for 1 minute, then drain and cool in a colander placed under running cold water. Whisk the oil and balsamic vinegar with some salt and pepper, and dress the sugar snaps.

Pack each dish in different sections of your lunchbox.

Get ahead
Make and pack up the day before, and store in the fridge.

Seafood chilli with tortilla bowls

Serves 8
(with some chilli
left over)

Preparation time:
30 minutes
(plus soaking time for
dried beans, if using)

Cooking time:
2 hours

I love spicy food. I try to sneak a bit of chilli on to almost everything I eat, from cheese on toast to a simple salad with a spicy dressing, or grilled fish with a good smear of chilli paste. Inevitably my chillies end up rather spicy too, so I always serve them with a cool dollop of sour cream to offset the heat.

400g dried black or turtle beans, or 3 x 400g tins of black beans, drained

vegetable oil

1 red onion, peeled and finely chopped

a bunch of spring onions, chopped and separated into green and white parts

2 dried chipotle chillies

6 cloves of garlic, peeled and crushed

2 tbsp tomato purée

1 tsp ground cumin

a pinch of ground cinnamon

1 tbsp paprika

2 x 400g tins of cherry tomatoes

2 corns on the cob or 1 x 200g tin of sweetcorn, drained

6 plain flour tortillas

200g pack of raw fish pie mix (chunks smoked haddock, salmon and cod)

200g seafood (prawns, squid and clams)

wedges of lime, to serve

For the soured cream sauce

200g soured cream

zest and juice of 1 lime

a pinch each of sea salt and sugar

If using dried beans, soak them overnight in plenty of cold water. Drain and give them a rinse. Place in a large saucepan of cold water and bring to the boil. Skim off any scum that floats to the surface and simmer for 1 hour. Leave them to cool in the water, then drain.

Heat a tablespoon of oil in a large saucepan over a medium heat, then add the red onion, white part of the spring onions, dried chillies and garlic. Fry for about 5 minutes, or until the onions are translucent and soft. Add the tomato purée, cumin, cinnamon and paprika and cook for 2 minutes, then add the tinned tomatoes. Fill both cherry tomato tins with water and pour into the saucepan.

Stir in the cooked beans and leave to simmer, uncovered, for 45 minutes. The sauce will reduce and thicken. (If using tinned beans, stir them in for the last 5 minutes.) Taste for seasoning and discard the chipotle chillies.

Meanwhile, mix the ingredients for the soured cream sauce together and set aside. Remove the leaves from the corn cobs. Cut off the sweetcorn (see tips) and set these aside too.

Preheat the oven to 160°C (fan). Place 6 ovenproof mugs or small bowls on a baking tray. Rub 2 tablespoons of oil on the tortillas and press them tightly oil side down into the mugs or bowls. Bake for 8–10 minutes, or until crisp and golden.

Five minutes before serving, heat a large non-stick pan with a tablespoon of oil. When hot, add the fish and cook for 2 minutes, shaking the pan to make sure the fish doesn't stick. Add the seafood and sweetcorn and cook for 3–4 minutes.

Stir and taste the tomato bean chilli for seasoning and reheat if necessary. Place a tortilla bowl on each plate and ladle in the chilli mix. Top with a dollop of sour cream, the seafood and sweetcorn, and sprinkle some of the green parts of the spring onions over. Serve immediately (to avoid the bowls becoming too soggy), with wedges of lime.

Tips

Place the tortillas in the microwave or oven for a few seconds if they are not pliable enough.

If you prefer the traditional mince, just add it to the onions at the beginning (making sure to brown it nicely before adding the rest of the ingredients).

To remove corn kernels from the cob, put a glass bowl on a dishcloth (to stop the bowl from slipping). Fold a piece of kitchen towel and place in the centre of the bowl. Rest one end of the corn cob on the kitchen towel and use a sharp knife to cut off the corn kernels, catching them all in the bowl.

Get ahead

The bean chilli is even better when made the day before (as the spices infuse the mix). Just fry the seafood and make the bowls before serving.

The soured cream sauce can also be made a day in advance.

Snap, crackle and pop fish

Serves
4

Preparation time:
20 minutes

Cooking time:
35 minutes

Fish, chips and mushy peas: a British gastronomic perennial. The paper wrap, the smell of malt vinegar and the crisp, golden battered fish ... Unfortunately, deep-frying at home is not as easy as it is at the chippie. I like to leave deep-frying to the professionals and avoid the havoc it can cause at home. A slick of grease down the hostess is particularly best avoided if you are cooking for guests.

I know what you are thinking ... puffed rice might be an odd thing to use, but it works miraculously well, giving the fish a crisp, crunchy coating without the greasy aftertaste and the guilt of a batter-drenched piece of fish.

1kg waxy potatoes (e.g. Bintje or Charlotte), scrubbed and dried well

4 tbsp olive oil

sea salt

400g frozen peas

a bunch of mint (20g), leaves and stalks separated

2 unwaxed lemons, zested and cut into wedges

8 heaped tbsp thick Greek yoghurt

freshly ground pepper

4 × 150g tail-end fillets of cod or pollack, skinned and deboned

4 tbsp plain flour

1 egg, beaten

60g puffed rice

2 tbsp rapeseed oil

tartare sauce (see page 249) and malt vinegar, to serve

Preheat the oven to 220°C (fan).

Cut the potatoes lengthways into 1cm thick chips, leaving the skin on. Place the chips in a large pan of cold water. Bring the water up to the boil, then cook for 1 minute before straining through a colander. The chips should still be uncooked and firm to the touch.

Put the chips on a large chopping board lined with kitchen towel and blot them dry. The drier they are, the crispier they will be after cooking. Line a tray with baking paper, put the chips on the tray and mix with the olive oil. Season with salt. Make sure the chips are spread in one layer only, then cook in the oven for 35 minutes, turning them every 10–15 minutes.

Meanwhile, prepare the mushy peas. Place the frozen peas, mint stalks, lemon zest and a couple of tablespoons of water in the pan, cover and cook for 5 minutes.

Discard the mint stalks. Roughly chop the mint leaves and put in a blender with the peas and the yoghurt. Blitz a few times until you have a chunky purée. Season with salt and pepper and add a squeeze of lemon. Transfer to a saucepan to keep warm until serving.

Season the fish fillets with salt and pepper. Set up 3 shallow bowls, one with the flour, one with the beaten egg and one with the puffed rice. Dip each piece of fish in the flour, then in the egg, then press firmly into the puffed rice to coat the fish well and evenly.

Put the rapeseed oil into a large non-stick pan on a medium heat. Add the fish fillets and fry on one side for 3–4 minutes, or until golden brown, then turn over and fry for a further 3–4 minutes.

Serve the crackling fish with the chips, mushy peas, tartare sauce and a wedge of lemon or splash of malt vinegar.

Smoked haddock hash with cornichon crème fraîche and salmon caviar

Serves 2 as a light lunch or 4 as a starter	Preparation time: 10 minutes	Cooking time: 25 minutes

If you cook in the same style as me, you probably verge on the over-generous side of portion control. So more often than not you are left with plenty of leftovers in your fridge. A hash is the perfect way of making sure none of that goes to waste and making leftovers go a bit further. I had a delicious one at a small café in East London; it was a ham hock hash topped with a sunshine orange fried egg. I've swapped ham for smoky haddock and the standard egg for some salmon caviar that pops in your mouth. But feel free to experiment with whatever is left in your fridge.

1 tbsp olive oil

1 onion, peeled and finely chopped

2 medium potatoes, scrubbed clean and cut into 1cm cubes

a pinch of sea salt

150g smoked haddock, skin removed and roughly chopped

black pepper, to taste

6 cornichons, finely chopped

3 tbsp crème fraîche

1 tsp lemon juice

4 tbsp salmon caviar

2 tbsp finely chopped chives

Heat a large frying pan with the oil and place over a medium heat. Once the oil is hot, add the onion, potatoes and a pinch of salt. Fry on a medium heat while stirring every so often for 20 minutes, or until tender. Add the haddock to the potatoes and fry for a further 5 minutes. Remove from the heat and season with plenty of black pepper.

In the meantime, mix the cornichons with the crème fraîche and lemon juice. Divide the potato mix between the plates and dot the cornichon crème fraîche and salmon caviar on top of the hash. Sprinkle each plate with plenty of chives.

Tip
Smoked haddock can be replaced with other smoked fish such as mackerel. If using smoked salmon omit the cooking process, cut into ribbons and garnish on top.

Speedy one-pot noodle

Serves
1

Preparation time:
3 minutes

Inspired by the classic Pot Noodle, this recipe is a gourmet version of the fastest of foods. You can jazz up this simple bowl of broth and noodles with all manner of meats and vegetables, then accessorize with fresh herbs, spices and seasonings. Here you have it: lunch in 3 minutes.

2–3 cubes of frozen reduced ham stock (see page 248) or hot vegetable stock (don't top up with the boiling water)

15g rice vermicelli noodles, broken up and soaked in boiling water for 1 minute, then drained

30g smoked tofu, sliced

3 fresh shiitake mushrooms, sliced

2 baby corn cobs, chopped

200ml boiling water

½ a small red chilli, deseeded and sliced

1 tbsp chopped fresh coriander or alfalfa and radish sprouts

2 spring onions, thinly sliced

optional: a pinch of togarashi* or chilli flakes

To serve

a squeeze of lime

fish sauce

light soy sauce

* a Japanese seasoning with chilli, orange, seaweed and sesame seeds

Place the ham stock, noodles, tofu, mushrooms and baby corn in the vessel you are serving from, then pour the boiling water over the top. Mix well and add the rest of the vegetables, herbs and spices. Serve with lime, fish sauce and soy to taste.

Variation

2–3 cubes of frozen reduced ham stock

15g rice vermicelli noodles, broken up and soaked in boiling water for 1 minute, then drained

1 tbsp tomato purée

1 tbsp Thai green curry paste

20g broccoli florets, blanched

30g roast chicken, shredded

30g red cabbage, shredded

Provençal roast chicken with roasted fennel

Serves	Preparation time:	Resting time:	Cooking time:
4	20 minutes	15–20 minutes	1 hour 20 minutes

A Sunday roast was a ritual in my house when I was a kid. My mum would spend ages in the kitchen preparing everything and making it perfect. The roasting smells wafting from the oven always made my stomach rumble.

This particular version was inspired by a visit to Provence, where olives sneak their way into numerous dishes (tapenade, *salade niçoise, pissaladière*) and the influence of nearby North Africa has introduced preserved lemons and the sweetness of sultanas to savoury dishes. This stuffing is an amalgamation of these flavours and makes for an effortlessly succulent roast chuck.

1.5kg whole free-range chicken (see tip if using larger)

4 bulbs of fennel, quartered, tough stems removed

2 onions, peeled and cut into quarters

50g sultanas

200ml white wine

a knob of soft butter

sea salt

For the stuffing

100g pitted green olives

5 preserved lemons (100g), drained, halved and pips removed

2 cloves of garlic, peeled

15g fresh flat-leaf parsley

a pinch of sea salt

freshly ground pepper

Preheat the oven to 180°C (fan).

In a food processor blend the olives, preserved lemons, garlic, parsley, salt and pepper to a paste. With your fingers, gently loosen the skin above the breast and legs of the chicken, keeping the skin intact but creating enough space to slip the stuffing right the way under.

Place the fennel and onions in a large roasting tin and scatter on the sultanas. Pour the wine into the tin. Place the chicken directly on top of the vegetables.

Rub the butter into the skin and scatter on some flaky sea salt. Roast breast side up for 1 hour and 20 minutes.

When the chicken has had the full cooking time, remove the tin from the oven and leave to rest for 10–15 minutes before transferring the chicken to a board to carve.

Serve the chicken with the braised fennel and onions and spoon over some of the roasting-tin juices (these are lovely and you don't want to waste them). Serve with the haricot bean salad on page 45.

Tip
If you have a larger or smaller chicken, work out the cooking time for your chicken based on this rule of thumb: 40 minutes per kg, plus 20 minutes.

Get ahead
You can make the stuffing the day before if you store it in the fridge.

Butternut snails with baby spinach and crispy mince

Serves	Preparation time:	Cooking time:
4	30 minutes	40 minutes

All you need to cook this is a frying pan. When I visited the Princes' Islands in Turkey, I met a lady called Buket, who runs a charming little bohemian café. Her kitchen is as tiny as the one I had in Paris, but she still manages to rustle up delicious treats for her customers. She also proves that you don't need an oven to make fantastic pastries – in her case, little rose-shaped ones filled with spinach. My versions look more like snails, and boast a hearty filling of butternut squash.

olive or vegetable oil

3 onions, peeled and finely chopped

350g butternut squash, peeled and cut into 1cm cubes

zest of ½ an orange

¼ tsp dried thyme

a pinch of ground cinnamon

sea salt and freshly ground pepper

100g fresh baby spinach, washed

8 large sheets of filo pastry

1 egg, plus 1 tbsp milk, beaten, for egg wash

For the spinach and crispy spiced mince salad

100g lamb mince

1 tbsp sumac

½ tsp chilli flakes

150g fresh baby spinach, washed

For the yoghurt dressing

150g plain yoghurt

juice and zest of ½ an orange

a pinch of sugar

Put 1 tablespoon of oil into a large frying pan. Add the onions and fry for 5 minutes before adding the butternut squash, orange zest, thyme and cinnamon. Season with salt and pepper, then cover and cook on a low heat for 15 minutes, or until the butternut is tender and the onions are soft. Throw in the spinach and stir, cover again and allow the spinach to wilt for 1 minute. Tip the filling on to a large plate and set it aside to cool completely.

Unroll a sheet of filo pastry horizontally on your work surface. Brush the filo with the egg wash, then put another sheet on top. Place a quarter of the stuffing in a thin line horizontally, about 4cm from the edge of the sheet, then start rolling the filo over the filling to cover. When you have a long, snake-like roll, roll it into a spiral to make a snail shape. Repeat with the rest of the filo to make 4 snails in total.

Put 1 tablespoon of oil into a large non-stick frying pan. Place the four snails in the pan and cook on a gentle heat for 15 minutes. Flip over halfway through. The snails should be nicely crisp on both sides.

Meanwhile, whisk together the yoghurt dressing ingredients, season with salt and pepper and set aside.

Mix together the mince, sumac and chilli flakes. When the snails are done, place on a plate and cover with aluminium foil to keep warm. Wipe the pan and put 1 tablespoon of oil into the pan. Place on a very high heat. When the pan begins to smoke, add the mince and turn the heat down to medium-high. Mash the mince with a wooden spoon to break it up, and cook for 4 minutes, or until crisp.

Assemble by placing a snail on a plate, followed by a small heap of fresh baby spinach. Drizzle with the yoghurt dressing and sprinkle with the crispy spiced mince. Serve immediately.

Tips

Wrap the snails really carefully in cling film if you are making them in advance, to stop the filo from drying out.

If you can't find sumac, replace with some freshly zested lemon and a pinch of paprika.

Get ahead

You can make the snails a few hours before serving, then just reheat in the oven at 150°C (fan) for 20 minutes.

Sticky chicken with Malaysian salad

Serves
4

Preparation time:
30 minutes

Cooking time:
45 minutes

Cucumber and pineapple is a traditional Malaysian salad, or *kerabu*, although it usually includes a fiery chilli. I took the chilli out so that the salad's cooling properties balance the spiciness of the chicken. The last time I had the salad was at the Malaysian Hall canteen in London, where homesick Malay students go to get their fill of home-cooking, just like mum makes it. The salad was so spicy it left my mouth numb.

1kg chicken drumsticks and thighs (approx. 4 of each)

1 tbsp sesame seeds, toasted

For the glaze

3 cloves of garlic, peeled

3cm ginger, peeled and roughly chopped

100g runny honey

80ml light soy sauce or tamari

1 red chilli, with seeds

2 tbsp sesame oil

2 tbsp fish sauce

For the Malaysian salad

1 cucumber, washed

½ a small pineapple

1 small red onion

juice of 1 lime

sea salt

Preheat the oven to 200°C (fan).

In a food processor, blend all the ingredients for the glaze together until fairly smooth.

When the oven is hot, place the chicken pieces in a large roasting tray with the glaze, tossing them well to coat. Bake for 45 minutes, remove from the oven and sprinkle with the toasted sesame seeds.

In the meantime, make the salad. Cut the cucumber in half lengthways, then deseed with a teaspoon and discard the seeds. Cut in half again, then slice across on the diagonal and put in a large bowl. Peel the pineapple, cut into small cubes and add this to the bowl. Peel and thinly slice the onion and add this too, along with the lime juice.

Taste and season the salad with salt just before serving.

Tips

If you want to bulk the meal up, serve with cooked basmati rice.

Make sure you season the salad with salt just before serving. If it's seasoned too far in advance, the salt will draw the moisture out of the cucumber, making the salad watery.

Get ahead

The uncooked chicken can be left in the glaze in the fridge for a couple of days before cooking.

Venison steak with celeriac purée, pickled blackberries and carrot petals

---

Serves	Preparation time:	Cooking time:
4	20 minutes	30 minutes

I have spent a great deal of time in Sweden over the last few years and developed an affinity to the flavours of the land. Sweden's long, cold winters have had a considerable impact on the national cuisine, bringing an abundance of root vegetables and game meat into the diet, and also influencing culinary techniques, such as pickling and smoking, which help preserve the food throughout the year.

The combination of berries with meat is not an unusual one. Lingonberry sauce is often served with game in Sweden, and regularly accompanies their perennial meatballs. Eating steak is not an everyday occasion for me. I prefer to eat less meat, but splash out when I do.

4 x 125–130g venison fillet steaks (3cm thick)

1 tbsp oil

sea salt and freshly ground pepper

a handful of chopped fresh mixed herbs (flat-leaf parsley, chives, dill)

For the celeriac purée

1 celeriac (600g), peeled

3–4 parsnips (400g), peeled

2 tbsp vegetable oil

100–150ml milk

2 knobs of soft butter

a pinch of freshly ground nutmeg

½ tsp white pepper

For the blackberries and carrots

50ml cider vinegar

100g granulated sugar

150ml water

1 tbsp sea salt

5 juniper berries, lightly bashed

10 black peppercorns

225g blackberries

2 small carrots

Equipment

a large ovenproof frying pan

Preheat the oven to 150°C (fan). Cut the celeriac and parsnips into 1cm cubes. Throw into a medium saucepan with the oil, stir and place on a medium heat. Cover tightly and cook for 15–20 minutes, or until tender, stirring regularly. Once cooked, place in a food processor and blend with the milk, bit by bit, then the butter. Add the nutmeg, pepper and a little salt and mix well.

In the meantime, make the pickle. In a medium saucepan stir together the cider vinegar, sugar, water, salt, juniper berries and peppercorns, and slowly bring to the boil. Once the sugar and salt have dissolved, take off the heat and leave to cool for 5 minutes before adding the blackberries. Set aside until needed.

Put a large ovenproof frying pan over a medium-high heat. Rub the oil all over the steaks and season them, then put them in the hot frying pan and cook for 1½–2 minutes on each side, or until they have a lovely dark crust.

Place the fillets in the oven in their pan for 5 minutes for medium. Place your serving plates in the oven at the same time to warm.

Peel the carrots and use a mandolin to make wafer-thin horizontal petals, or cut the carrots in half vertically and shave off petals with a speed peeler. Take a couple of tablespoons of the pickling liquid and toss the carrot petals in it.

Take the steaks out of the oven. Cover with aluminium foil and leave to rest for 5 minutes. When the meat has rested, transfer to a board and cut the steaks into thin slices.

To serve, put a generous dollop of purée on to each plate, followed by several slices of venison and a little of the meat juices from the steaks. Finish by spooning the pickled blackberries and carrots on top and around the plate. Garnish with the herbs of your choice.

Tips

Take the steaks out of the fridge at least 30 minutes before cooking them.

Cooking the celeriac with no water and only a little oil allows it to cook in its own juices. There's no water to dilute the taste. Pass the purée through a sieve or ricer for an extra-smooth texture.

Get ahead

The pickled blackberries will keep in an air-tight container or jar in the fridge for a couple of weeks.

Shepherdless pie

Serves 4–6	Preparation time: 30 minutes	Cooking time: 40 minutes

Shepherd's pie is one of my favourite British dishes, and I often made it in my days au-pairing for a French family in Paris. I've adapted it by using Puy lentils, from the Auvergne region in France; they keep their shape and have a great bite, making them a perfect mince substitute.

Making shepherd's pie can be a bit time-consuming if you have to make mashed potatoes (although it's a great way of using leftovers). So I've simplified it by using a creamy polenta topping that is crisped up in the oven – meaning less time in the kitchen and more time to put your feet up (or get all those other tasks done).

200g dried Puy or beluga lentils

2 lapsang souchong tea bags

1 tbsp rapeseed oil

1 onion, peeled and finely chopped

1 carrot, peeled and diced

10 cherry tomatoes, finely chopped

1 tbsp sweet smoked paprika

8 mushrooms, roughly chopped

2 tbsp tomato purée

2 tsp Marmite or yeast extract

sea salt and freshly ground pepper

For the creamy polenta topping

800ml vegetable stock

1 tbsp fresh thyme leaves

1 tbsp finely chopped fresh parsley

200g instant polenta flour

1 tbsp rapeseed oil

Equipment

a deep 26cm x 20cm baking dish

Place the lentils and tea bags in a medium saucepan. Cover with a litre of cold water and bring to the boil, then turn the heat down and simmer for 20–25 minutes or until al dente. Drain the lentils, saving 200ml of the cooking liquid, and discard the tea bags.

Preheat the grill to medium-high.

Put the oil into a large frying pan and add the onion, carrot, tomatoes and paprika. Fry gently for 10 minutes, or until the onion is translucent. Add the mushrooms and cook for a further 5 minutes, stirring frequently.

Add the cooked lentils with the 200ml of cooking liquid, the tomato purée and Marmite. Stir until the tomato purée and Marmite have dissolved, then cook for 2 minutes. Taste and season with salt and pepper. Take off the heat and cover while making the polenta.

Put the vegetable stock and herbs in a large saucepan and bring to the boil. When boiling, add the polenta in a slow stream, stirring continuously for a couple of minutes until the mixture thickens and bubbles. Stir in the oil and take off the heat. Taste for seasoning.

Pour the lentil filling into the baking dish and spread the hot polenta on the top. Use a fork to make lines on the top; this helps to make it crispier. Place under the grill for 5–10 minutes, or until the top crisps up.

Tip

Stir the polenta constantly with a wooden spoon or large balloon whisk to prevent lumps building up. If it is thickening too quickly, remove from the heat and beat very hard.

Cauliflower cheese burgers

<table>
<tr><td>Serves
6</td><td>Preparation time:
20 minutes</td><td>Cooking time:
25 minutes</td></tr>
</table>

The burger craze doesn't seem to have left a stone unturned. New York, London, Paris, Stockholm: every city I visit has any number of burger bars touting gourmet beef patties in soft brioche buns. Don't get me wrong, I love a burger! But after seeing all that meat I find myself craving something a little lighter and fresher tasting. Wrap your hand round this cauliflower cheeseburger, take a big bite and let some of the burger juice dribble down your hand . . . just like the real deal!

1 very small head of cauliflower (approx. 200g), trimmed and separated into florets

140g tinned haricot beans (drained weight)

85g fresh breadcrumbs

140g mature Cheddar cheese

2 tablespoons chopped fresh flat-leaf parsley

a sprinkling of grated nutmeg

zest of 1 unwaxed lemon

1 tablespoon roasted chopped hazelnuts

sea salt and freshly ground pepper

1 large egg white

2 tbsp vegetable or olive oil

1 oak leaf lettuce (or other)

1 medium tomato, sliced

For the caramelized onion chutney (makes 250g)

50g butter

4 red onions, peeled and thinly sliced

a pinch of sea salt

150ml red wine vinegar

2 tbsp raisins, finely chopped

2 tbsp soft brown sugar

Steam the cauliflower florets for 7–8 minutes, or until tender. Take off the heat, drain and leave in the colander to cool.

In the meantime, start to make the red onion chutney. Put the butter in a frying pan on a low heat, then add the onions and salt. Fry for about 20 minutes, or until sticky and soft. Add the vinegar, raisins and sugar, and cook for another 5 minutes, or until glossy and reduced. Check the seasoning.

When the cauliflower is cool, put the haricot beans into a food processor and pulse, then add the cauliflower and pulse lightly. You don't want to overwork it as the mixture will get sloppy. Place in a bowl and add 1 tbsp of breadcrumbs. Grate 80g of the Cheddar and add to the bowl, along with the parsley, nutmeg, lemon zest and hazelnuts. Season with salt and pepper, and form the mix into 6 patties, around 6cm in diameter each, in the palms of your hands.

Lightly whisk the egg white in a bowl, and put the rest of the breadcrumbs on to a plate. Brush each patty all over with egg white and press into the crumbs, making sure they are well covered.

Put the oil into a large frying pan on a medium-high heat. When hot, cook the patties in batches for 3–4 minutes on each side, until nice and crisp and golden. Slice the remaining Cheddar and put a slice on top of each patty while in the pan to melt. Place each patty in a lettuce leaf, add a slice of tomato and serve with a generous spoonful of chutney.

Tip
Serve with toasted open pitta bread or brioche bun if you want a more 'classic' burger.

Get ahead
You can freeze these patties on a tray, before coating in the egg white and breadcrumbs. Then defrost, coat, and fry in a pan, as above.

Duck ragù with crisp porridge wedges

Serves	Preparation time:	Cooking time:	Chilling time:
4	30 minutes	2 hours	30 minutes minimum

I have an enduring love of porridge and it doesn't stop at breakfast. I grew up with savoury porridge for dinner. My mum, an ever-so-thrifty cook, made an Asian-style porridge using leftover rice and roast chicken, spiked with chilli, ginger and spring onions. Serving porridge for dinner might not be the most obvious choice, but pan-fry it to crisp and golden perfection and you'll end up with the most amazing accompaniment to a rich ragù.

For the orange duck ragù

3 duck legs

sea salt and freshly ground pepper

1 tbsp sunflower oil

4 cloves of garlic, peeled and finely minced

2 tinned anchovy fillets, drained and chopped

1 onion, peeled and finely chopped

2 carrots, peeled and roughly chopped

1 stick of celery, roughly chopped

150ml red wine

1 x 400g tin of cherry tomatoes

1 large sprig of rosemary

zest of 1 orange, removed in strips using a vegetable peeler

For the crisp porridge wedges

200g rolled porridge oats

250ml milk

350ml hot chicken stock

3 tbsp finely chopped chives

60g Parmesan cheese, finely grated

2 tbsp butter

Equipment

a 20cm x 20cm baking tin, lined with cling film

Season the duck legs with plenty of salt and pepper. Put the oil into a large lidded saucepan on a medium heat. When hot, place the duck legs in the pan, skin side down, and fry for 3 minutes, or until the skin begins to go golden and crisp. Turn over and cook for a further 2 minutes. Remove from the pan and place on a plate.

Lower the heat and add the garlic, anchovies, onion, carrots and celery. Fry uncovered for about 5 minutes, or until the anchovies have disintegrated, then add the wine. Simmer for 2 minutes, then add the tomatoes, rosemary and orange zest. Bring back to a simmer, add the browned duck legs, then cover and cook on a low heat for about 1½ hours, or until the meat is tender and falling off the bone. Discard the orange zest and rosemary. Transfer the duck legs to a board and, using two forks, shred the duck meat, discarding the skin and bones. Stir the duck meat back into the tomato sauce and taste for seasoning.

Meanwhile, place the oats in a medium saucepan with the milk and stock. Leave to soak for 10 minutes, then place on a medium-low heat and bring to a simmer while stirring continously with a wooden spoon or spatula. When the porridge is thick and unctuous, take off the heat. Stir in most of the chives (saving the rest for the garnish), the Parmesan and some salt and pepper, and stir well to combine. Pour the porridge into your lined tin and spread evenly across the base. Refrigerate for a minimum of 30 minutes.

Put 1 tablespoon of butter into a large frying pan on a high heat. Cut the porridge into 4 slices and place them in the hot pan. Fry each slice on both sides, about 6−7 minutes in total, until golden.

Place a porridge slice on each serving plate and top with the ragù and a sprinkle of chives.

Stir-fried cauliflower rice

Serves	Preparation time:	Cooking time:
4	20 minutes	10 minutes

I'm a firm believer in the mantra 'butter makes everything better', but there are some days when I fancy something a touch lighter. True to my Asian roots, I regularly rustle up a stir-fry from a fridge raid of leftovers when I want a quick bite; using cauliflower as a rice substitute makes the dish even healthier.

1 small head of cauliflower (approx. 300g), trimmed and separated into florets

4 spring onions, whites and green parts separated and finely chopped

10 baby sweetcorn, cut into rounds

1 red pepper, deseeded and cut into thin strips

2 tbsp sunflower oil

4 eggs

a pinch each of white pepper and sea salt

1 red chilli, deseeded and finely chopped

4 cloves of garlic, peeled and finely minced

1 thumb-sized piece of ginger, peeled and grated

30g cashew nuts, roughly chopped

4 tbsp light soy sauce or tamari

1 lime, quartered, to serve

Place the cauliflower in a blender or food processor and pulse to breadcrumb consistency. Put into a bowl, add the white parts of the spring onions, the baby sweetcorn and red pepper, and mix.

Place a large (approx. 26cm) non-stick frying pan with 1 tablespoon of oil on a medium heat. Crack the eggs into a bowl and beat with the pepper and salt. Pour the eggs into the pan and swirl the pan around, so the mixture covers the whole base. Cook for a couple of minutes, or until the eggs are set, then flip over and cook for a further 1–2 minutes, or until just set. Slide the omelette on to a chopping board, leave to cool slightly, then roll up and cut into 1cm-wide strips. Set aside until needed.

Put the remaining tablespoon of oil into a wok or large frying pan on a medium heat. When it gets hot, add the chilli, garlic, ginger and cashew nuts. Cook for 30 seconds while continuously tossing in the hot oil. Add the cauliflower rice, sweetcorn and pepper. Continue tossing for 3–4 minutes, until it's nicely golden. Add the sliced omelette and stir to heat through, then pour the soy sauce into the pan and toss well before dividing between bowls. Serve each with a wedge of lime and sprinkling of the green tops from the spring onions.

Tips

Use a teaspoon to scrape the skin off the ginger.

Use tamari instead of regular soy sauce to make this gluten-free.

Stir-frying is an excellent way of using up anything left over in the fridge, from roast meat to veg.

Mushroom stroganoff with spinach and wild rice

Serves
4

Preparation time:
15 minutes

Cooking time:
30 minutes

I have a fond memory of stroganoff, since it was often served for dinner at home when I was a kid. My mum has always been a classic cook, so we had beef stroganoff rather than my vegetarian version. Portobello mushrooms are a popular meat substitute in vegetarian cooking; they are dense, chewy and have a deep, intense flavour. I think they can match beef or chicken any day, and for a fraction of the price.

200g wild red rice (I like Camargue)

sea salt

100g baby spinach

1 tbsp butter

4 extra-large portobello mushrooms, stems removed (or 8 smaller ones)

3 cloves of garlic, peeled and minced

400ml hot vegetable stock

2 tsp cornflour

150ml whole milk

2 tbsp Dijon mustard

freshly ground pepper

zest and juice of ½ an unwaxed lemon

2 heaped tbsp cornichons, finely chopped

2 sprigs of dill, finely chopped

Cook the wild rice in salted boiling water in a medium saucepan according to packet instructions. Once cooked, drain and place back in the saucepan with the baby spinach. Stir through, so the spinach wilts, then cover and set aside until needed.

Put the butter into a large frying or sauté pan on a medium heat. Add the mushrooms with the flat caps facing down and fry until soft and beginning to brown. Flip them over and cook for several minutes, then add the garlic. Place the vegetable stock in a medium saucepan and simmer on a medium heat.

In a separate bowl, mix the cornflour with 2 tablespoons of the milk to make a smooth paste. Whisk it into the hot stock, along with the Dijon mustard, pepper to taste and the remaining milk. Add it to the mushrooms (beware, as it may splutter). Simmer for 2 minutes, then remove the mushrooms from the pan and set aside, covering them with aluminium foil to keep warm. Turn up the heat under the pan and whisk the sauce for about 15 minutes, or until it has the consistency of single cream. Take off the heat, squeeze in the lemon juice and taste for seasoning.

Serve each mushroom on a bed of spinach wild rice. Spoon over the sauce and garnish with the cornichons, the lemon zest and the dill.

Tip
The mushrooms can be replaced with 600g of beef or chicken. Cut into thin strips or bite-sized pieces and add at the same stage of the recipe as the mushrooms. Fry for about 10 minutes, stirring regularly.

Get ahead
You can make the sauce and fry the mushrooms in advance, then reheat on a low heat.

Chicken salad with buttermilk dressing and chicken skin croutons

---

Serves
4

Preparation time:
15 minutes

Cooking time:
35 minutes

Iceberg lettuce went out of fashion some time ago, losing to a bag of pre-washed mixed leaves. But it's definitely making a comeback. Wedges of iceberg are now popping up on restaurant menus, reminding us that there's something ever so refreshing about the crunchy fresh lettuce that no spindly rocket leaf, radicchio or baby red chard can fulfil. This is my salad of choice on a hot day.

100ml water

100g caster sugar

1 lemon, thinly sliced, pips removed

2 large skin-on chicken breasts

sea salt

4 tsp Dijon mustard

2 tsp rapeseed oil

100ml buttermilk (or 70ml yoghurt and 30ml milk)

1 small clove of garlic, peeled

4 tinned anchovy fillets, drained

2 sticks of celery, trimmed

1 head of iceberg lettuce, quartered and washed

½ a cucumber, thinly sliced into rounds

2 tbsp finely chopped chives

2 tbsp capers, drained (rinsed if salted)

Preheat the oven to 200°C (fan). Place the water and sugar in a medium saucepan on a high heat and bring to the boil. Place the lemon slices in a heatproof bowl. Once the sugar has dissolved and the syrup has boiled for 1 minute, pour over the lemon. Set aside to cool until needed.

Remove the skin from the chicken breasts. Place the skin on a baking tray lined with baking paper, sprinkle with salt and bake in the oven for 30 minutes, or until golden and crisp. Remove from the tray and place on kitchen towel. Cut into small pieces.

Meanwhile, heat a griddle pan until very hot. Butterfly the chicken breasts by placing on a chopping board, then using a sharp knife to slice each one horizontally, starting from the straighter side. Don't cut all the way through: leave the edge in place, so that you can open them up like a book. Set aside on a plate, then take 2 pieces of cling film that are 3 times bigger than an open fillet. Lay 1 piece of cling film on the board, place an open fillet on top and cover with the second piece of film. Use a rolling pin to bash the chicken to about 0.5cm thick. Repeat with the other fillet.

Remove the chicken from the cling film. Spread the Dijon mustard on both sides, drizzle with oil and sprinkle with salt. Place 1 fillet on the griddle pan once it's smoky hot and cook for 2 minutes on each side. Do this in 2 batches. Remove the chicken from the heat and leave to rest for 5 minutes, then slice into thin strips.

Blend the buttermilk, garlic and anchovies using a hand-held blender or a food processor. Use a speed-peeler to make ribbons from the long lengths of the celery. Divide the iceberg lettuce between four bowls. Add the strips of chicken, cucumber and celery, then drizzle over the buttermilk dressing. Sprinkle with the crispy chicken skin, chives, capers and some of the drained candied lemon slices.

Tip
This dish also makes a great side salad if you leave the chicken out and slice the iceberg lettuce into strips.

Get ahead
The candied lemon slices can be made up to 1 week in advance and stored in an airtight container in the fridge. You can substitute them for preserved lemons, finely sliced.

Onion petal spätzle

Serves 4	Preparation time: 15 minutes	Cooking time: 60 minutes

Spätzle — little button dumplings — are something I grew up with, having an Austrian mum. They're usually tossed in butter and served with grated cheese, but I serve them with dry-roasted onions, which gives the dish a lovely sweetness. This technique is inspired by our Nordic gastro-trendsetters, who know a thing or two about alliums.

6 brown onions, unpeeled and quartered

8 cloves of garlic, unpeeled

40g soft butter, plus a knob for frying

2 shallots, peeled and quartered

2 eggs

60g fresh parsley

sea salt and freshly ground pepper

140g plain flour

a handful of chopped mixed fresh herbs such as parsley, thyme, oregano and basil

100g Parmesan or other mature hard cheese, grated

Preheat the oven to 180°C (fan). Place the onions and 6 cloves of garlic skin side down in a roasting tray. Roast for 30 minutes, or until soft and golden.

Peel the remaining 2 cloves of garlic and put them in a food processor, along with the butter, shallots, eggs, parsley and ½ a teaspoon each of salt and pepper. Blend to a smooth paste, remove from the blender and beat in the flour.

Place a colander on top of a saucepan of simmering salted water (don't let the colander touch the water). Pour in the batter and use a spatula to push it through the holes, making miniature dumplings. Cook for 2 minutes, then drain.

Peel the skins from the roasted onions and cut the root off, then pull the onion layers apart, into petals. Put a knob of butter into a large frying pan on a medium heat. When the butter has melted, turn the heat down to low and add the chopped herbs and onion petals. Cut one end off the roasted cloves of garlic and squeeze the garlic into the frying pan, discarding the skin. When the butter begins to brown, take off the heat and toss in the *spätzle*. Season, then scatter the cheese on top and serve immediately.

Tips

If you don't have any fresh herbs, you can use 1 tablespoon of dried herbs instead.

If you have some white wine left over (roughly 100ml), add this to the pan before adding the spätzle. Turn up the heat and reduce by half, then add the spätzle.

Get ahead

The onions and garlic can be roasted in advance and heated in the pan with the butter.

Pickled pear, lentil and gorgonzola salad

Serves	Preparation time:	Resting time:	Cooking time:
4	15 minutes	overnight	1 hour

That wholesome image that lentils conjure up always leaves me with a smug glow in the aftermath of eating – quite unlike pasta or rice, which can leave you feeling bloated. After living in France, there's only one kind of lentil I like to eat (call me a lentil snob if you like) and that's the Puy. It keeps its shape and doesn't end up mushy. Puy lentils are easy to top with an endless combination of ingredients or can be thrown into a salad to give it some bite. Don't let your lentils get pushed to the back of the cupboard!

4 small beetroots (350g in total), peeled and cut into 2cm cubes

250ml water

250ml red wine vinegar

150g caster sugar

4 firm pears (I like Conference), peeled but with the stalk on

200g Puy lentils

100g Gorgonzola, Dolcelatte or other blue cheese

50g watercress

2 tbsp extra virgin olive oil

sea salt and freshly ground pepper

Pour the water, vinegar and sugar into a small saucepan (the pears should sit snugly) and bring to a gentle simmer. Stir to dissolve the sugar, then add the pears and beetroot. Take a piece of baking paper larger than the diameter of the pan, crumple it up and cut a hole or slit in the centre. Place in contact with the liquid and let some seep through to keep the paper in place. Cover and simmer gently on a low heat for an hour.

Remove from the heat and place the pears, beetroot and all the liquid in a separate container. Leave to cool to room temperature, then put in the fridge and leave to pickle overnight.

When ready to eat, cook the lentils following the packet instructions, then drain. Remove the pears from the container to a chopping board and transfer the beetroot to a bowl (discard the liquid or save it for pickling something else). Toss the lentils with the beetroot, then crumble the blue cheese into small chunks and add this to the bowl.

Divide the mixture between 4 plates. Cut each pear in half and place 2 halves on each plate, with a little watercress on top. Drizzle with the oil and sprinkle with a pinch each of salt and pepper.

Tips

It's important that the pears are large, firm and not overripe, otherwise they will become mushy and disintegrate when cooked.

You can use any other soft cheese, such as goat's cheese or feta, to replace the blue cheese.

Get ahead

The longer the pears and beetroot sit in the pickling juices, the darker the colour and the stronger the flavour.

Chicory, blood orange and scallop salad

Serves
2 as a light lunch
or 4 as a starter

Preparation time:
10 minutes

Cooking time:
under 5 minutes

I love a colourful plate of food, especially on a dreary winter's day. Luckily, even in the winter months you can add some colour to your plate with red chicory and blood oranges. They just happen to be in season at the same time, and there couldn't be a better match. Bitter chicory and sweet-and-sour blood oranges are not just the ultimate colour combo but a perfect palate pairing too.

4 blood oranges

2 tbsp extra virgin olive oil

2 heads of red chicory, ends trimmed and leaves separated

sea salt and freshly ground pepper

8 scallops with roes (removed from the fridge 15 minutes before cooking)

1 tbsp olive oil

1 tbsp butter

20 green olives, pitted and finely chopped

2 tbsp finely chopped chives

Top and tail the oranges with a paring knife, then place upright on the chopping board and slice away the skin and pith, discarding these. Cut between the membranes to remove the individual segments of orange, then place in a bowl. Squeeze the juice from the remaining 'skeleton' of the membranes into a salad bowl.

Add the extra virgin olive oil to the orange juice in the salad bowl and whisk.

Add the chicory leaves, toss to dress and season with salt and pepper.

Peel away the tough crescent-shaped tendon from the outside of the scallops. Dab the scallops with kitchen towel to remove any moisture, and season well with salt and pepper on both sides.

Put a large non-stick frying pan over a medium heat and pour in the olive oil. When the pan is hot, add the scallops. Sear on the first side for 1–2 minutes (depending on their size), without moving, so that they get a nice crust. Then add 1 tbsp of butter to the pan, flip the scallops over and cook for 1 further minute, tilting the pan on its side and spooning the butter over.

Scatter the leaves on a serving plate or individual plates, followed by the orange segments and the green olives. Place the scallops on top and sprinkle with the chives.

Tip
The scallops can be replaced with 150g of salty, creamy goat's cheese.

Get ahead
You can segment the oranges and make the dressing a few hours in advance.

Summer spaghetti bolognese

Serves	Preparation time:	Cooking time:
4	15 minutes	15 minutes

There are a few things I try to grow in my window boxes, and herbs, radishes and salad are a must. One year I grew cherry tomatoes, which proved such a success that I couldn't pick them quickly enough. My neighbours complained that tomatoes would fall on their heads when they walked into the main entrance below. I didn't intend to bomb my neighbours with tomatoes, so now I keep my urban gardening to herbs and leafy greens, which are easy to maintain. This recipe really relies on a bounty of summer tomatoes to bring it alive. Unlike the classic spaghetti bolognese, which benefits from a slow, gentle simmer, this is a quick, fresh alternative.

500g mixed tomatoes (different colours and sizes)

1 small red onion, peeled and thinly sliced

1 tbsp extra virgin olive oil

2 tbsp rapeseed oil

1 brown onion, peeled and finely chopped

4 cloves of garlic, peeled and crushed

200g lamb's liver, finely chopped

8 slices of smoked streaky bacon, finely chopped

1 tbsp chopped fresh thyme leaves, plus extra to garnish

1 tbsp chopped fresh oregano leaves, plus extra to garnish

400g spaghetti

1 tbsp tomato purée

3 tbsp red wine vinegar

sea salt and freshly ground pepper

Cut the tomatoes into quarters or halves, depending on the size. Toss with the red onion and extra virgin olive oil and set aside.

Put the rapeseed oil, brown onion, garlic, liver and bacon into a large frying pan on a medium heat. Add the herbs and fry for 10 minutes, or until the onion and meat begin to brown nicely, stirring constantly.

In the meantime, bring a large pot of salted water to the boil and cook the pasta according to the packet instructions. Drain in a colander, setting aside some of the pasta water. Stir in the tomato purée and red wine vinegar. Taste and season with salt and pepper.

Toss the liver and bacon with the tomatoes and pasta and loosen with 1 or 2 tablespoons of the pasta water. Pour into a large serving dish, sprinkle the extra herbs on top, and serve immediately.

Tip
The liver and bacon can be replaced with beef, lamb or pork mince.

Get ahead
The liver and onion mixture can be made a day ahead. Simply reheat in a pan with 1 tablespoon of oil.

Courgette linguine
with three different sauces

Serves	Preparation time:	Cooking time:
4	10 minutes	15 minutes

I'm one to break the rules, and when it comes to pasta I say no to flour and yes to vegetables. Homemade pasta doesn't have to contain flour or be tricky to make, and courgette linguine is perfect for your gluten-intolerant friends. All you need is some courgettes and a julienne peeler, spiralizer or a mandolin.

I returned from my travels craving vegetables and something a little lighter. I can be pretty lazy when it comes to cooking for myself, and these pasta dishes can all be rustled up in minutes.

Tip
Courgette linguine is best eaten immediately, as it gets soggy if you reheat it.

Get ahead
The three sauces can all be made up to 2 days in advance.

with frozen pea and dill pesto

150g frozen petit pois or garden peas

10g fresh dill

a pinch each of sugar and sea salt

2 tbsp water

50g Parmesan cheese or other mature hard cheese, finely grated, plus extra to serve

2 tbsp lemon juice

freshly ground pepper

4 courgettes

1 tbsp butter

Place the peas in a small lidded saucepan. Strip the dill leaves from the stalks and add the stalks to the pan with the sugar and salt. Add the water, place the lid on the pan, bring to the boil and cook for 2 minutes. Remove the lid, check the peas are tender, then pour the contents of the pan into a food processor. Add the dill leaves, Parmesan, lemon juice and pepper, and blend the mixture – I like to keep it a bit textured. Check the seasoning.

Use a julienne peeler, spiralizer or a mandolin with a julienne blade to make long ribbons down the length of the courgettes, discarding the seedy core. Put the butter into a large lidded pan on a medium heat and add the courgette linguine. Place the lid on the pan and sweat the courgette for 1–2 minutes, until softened. Drain off any excess liquid, return to the pan and toss with the pea and dill pesto. Serve with an extra grating of Parmesan.

with walnut and sage sauce

75g walnuts

50g salted butter

10g sage leaves

3–4 tbsp water

1 tbsp lemon juice

sea salt and freshly ground pepper

1 tbsp butter

4 courgettes

Place a non-stick frying pan over a medium-high heat. When hot, put the walnuts into the pan and dry-fry for 5 minutes, or until they smell toasted, then remove and set aside. Put the butter into the pan on a medium heat and add the sage leaves. Cook for about 3 minutes, or until the butter starts to brown and the leaves begin to crisp up. Take off the heat and place in a food processor. Add the toasted walnuts, water, lemon juice, and salt and pepper to taste, and blend to a purée.

Use a julienne peeler, spiralizer or a mandolin with a julienne blade to make long ribbons down the length of the courgettes, discarding the seedy core. Put the butter into a large lidded pan on a medium heat and add the courgette linguine. Place the lid on the pan and sweat the courgette for 1–2 minutes, until softened. Drain off any excess liquid, return to the pan and toss with the walnut and sage sauce.

with tomato, olive and caper sauce

1 tbsp olive oil

3 cloves of garlic, peeled and finely minced

1 x 400g tin of cherry tomatoes

4 courgettes

10 black olives, pitted and chopped

2 tbsp capers, drained (rinsed if salted)

a pinch of sea salt

70g Parmesan cheese or other mature hard cheese, to serve

Put the oil into a large pan over a low heat. Add the garlic and fry gently for 1 minute, then add the cherry tomatoes with their juice and simmer for 10 minutes.

In the meantime, make the linguine. Use a julienne peeler, spiralizer or a mandolin with a julienne blade to make long ribbons down the length of the courgettes, discarding the seedy core.

Crush the cherry tomato sauce with a fork and stir in the black olives and capers. Season with the salt, then take off the heat and toss the courgettes in the sauce for around 1 minute, or until coated thoroughly and warmed through.

Plate up the courgette linguine, then grate the Parmesan over the top. Serve with mini focaccia buns (see page 251) to mop up the sauce.

Puff pastry pies

Makes 6 pie cases (each pie serves 1)	Preparation time: 15 minutes	Cooking time: 25–30 minutes

If there's one thing I keep in my freezer, it's not a tub of ice cream: it's a roll of all butter puff pastry. It's great to have as a backup for all sorts of things, from little aperitif snacks in the form of twisted cheese straws to these immensely versatile puff pastry pies.

Tip
These puff pastry pies can be filled with anything you fancy, as long as the filling isn't too soggy.

2 x 320g packs of ready-rolled all butter puff pastry (remove from fridge 15 minutes before using)

1 egg, beaten, for egg wash

Preheat the oven to 180°C (fan). Unroll the pastry carefully from the paper. Cut six 10cm squares with a long knife or pizza cutter, then use the remaining pastry to cut 48 strips of pastry 2cm wide and 10cm long (you may need to re-roll the last pieces for the final strips). Brush the squares with the egg wash, then stick a pastry strip on each edge of the squares to make a border. Top each of the borders with another layer of pastry strips, then brush again with egg wash and place the squares on a baking tray lined with baking paper. Put in the oven and bake for 25–30 minutes, or until golden, crisp and puffy.

You can either make the pie cases at the same time as the fillings below, or make the cases up to 3 days in advance and store them in an airtight container until ready to use. Reheat for 15 minutes at 160°C (fan).

Roasted baby vegetable pie filling

For
6 pies

Preparation time:
5 minutes

Cooking time:
30 minutes

12 baby courgettes

12 baby carrots

12 baby parsnips

1 tbsp olive oil

6 tsp sun-dried tomato paste

2 tbsp extra virgin olive oil

sea salt

Preheat the oven to 180°C (fan). Cut the vegetables in half horizontally. Put them into a small baking dish and toss with the olive oil, then roast in the oven for around 30 minutes, or until tender.

Smear the sun-dried tomato paste on the base of each pie case. Arrange the vegetables upright in the pie case, then drizzle with the extra virgin olive oil and sprinkle over a little salt.

Tuna, sweetcorn and caper pie filling

For
6 pies

Preparation time:
5 minutes

2 x 200g tins of good-quality tuna, drained (300g drained weight), or 2 x 70g fillets of smoked trout, flaked

100g tinned sweetcorn, drained

1 tbsp capers, roughly chopped

4 cornichons, roughly chopped

6 tbsp mayonnaise (see page 249)

In a small bowl, mix together the tuna or trout, sweetcorn, capers and cornichons. Divide between the pie cases and dot the mayonnaise on the top.

Roasted sausage, apple and onion pie filling

For 6 pies	Preparation time: 5 minutes	Cooking time: 30–40 minutes

3 small onions, peeled and quartered

6 free-range pork sausages

1 tbsp olive oil

6 medium apples

6 tsp English mustard

Preheat the oven to 180°C (fan). Place the onions and sausages in a large roasting tray and drizzle over the oil, tossing to coat. Wrap each of the apples in a piece of aluminium foil and place in the roasting tray. Roast for 30–40 minutes, or until the sausages are golden and cooked through and the onions are soft.

Remove the tray from the oven. Wearing a clean pair of rubber gloves, carefully remove the apples from the aluminium foil and mash the flesh with a fork, discarding the skin and core. Spread 1 teaspoon of mustard in the base of each pie case, and divide the mashed apple between the cases. Cut each sausage in half and arrange in the bases, along with 2 onion quarters per pie. Serve immediately.

Caramelized plum filling

For 6 pies	Preparation time: 5 minutes	Cooking time: 20 minutes

a knob of butter

1 tbsp light brown sugar

9 smallish plums

2 tbsp lemon juice

Put a medium lidded non-stick frying pan on a medium-low heat. Put the butter and sugar in the pan and let them melt for 2 minutes. Cut the plums in half, gouge the stone out if you can (if you can't, you can do this more easily once they are cooked), and place flesh side down in the pan. Cook for 5 minutes, then add the lemon juice and spoon the sauce over the plums. Place a lid on the pan and cook for a further 10 minutes, or until they are tender but holding their shape. Place 3 halves in each of the pie cases and spoon over the pan juices. Serve with a dollop of crème fraîche, whipped cream or ice cream.

Caramelized plum filling

Roasted baby vegetable pie filling

Tuna, sweetcorn and capers pie filling

Roasted sausage, apple and onion pie filling

Aubergine and halloumi schnitzel with stewed tomatoes

Serves	Preparation time:	Salting time:	Cooking time:
4	10 minutes	15 minutes minimum	1 hour

Schnitzel was always a special treat at home when I was a kid. Golden crisp crumbs encasing a juicy veal escalope, with a dollop of ketchup on the side: just thinking of it makes me salivate a little. I'm not someone who believes a dinner plate is incomplete without a carnivorous centrepiece, however. The meaty texture of aubergine lends itself very well to being coated in breadcrumbs and halloumi, while the stewed tomatoes are a sophisticated, grown-up homage to my childhood love of ketchup.

350g cherry tomatoes

2 small red onions, peeled and finely sliced

5 sprigs of fresh thyme, plus a few extra leaves to serve

2 tbsp red wine vinegar

2 tbsp extra virgin olive oil

sea salt and freshly ground pepper

1 large aubergine

1 tbsp vegetable oil

1 large egg

100g fresh white breadcrumbs

70g halloumi cheese, finely grated

½ tsp dried mint

Preheat the oven 200°C (fan).

Place the tomatoes in a baking dish with the onion slices, sprigs of thyme, vinegar, extra virgin olive oil and some salt and pepper. Stir well, and bake in the oven for 40 minutes, giving everything another stir 20 minutes into the cooking time.

In the meantime, remove and discard the stalk from the aubergine, Slice the aubergine lengthways into 1cm-thick slices, and slice the skin off the small end lengths (this will help the crumbs to stick). Sprinkle with salt on both sides and leave to sit in a colander for 15 minutes. Rinse well, then dab off the excess moisture with a clean tea towel.

Pour the vegetable oil into a large baking dish and place in the oven to heat up. Whisk the egg and place in a shallow bowl. Mix the breadcrumbs, halloumi and dried mint together on a large plate. Set a clean plate on one side. Dip each aubergine slice into the egg, then press into the breadcrumbs on both sides and place on the clean plate.

Remove the baking dish from the oven and place the slices side by side in the oil. Press any leftover crumbs on to the top of the slices. Bake for 20–25 minutes, or until both sides are golden and crispy.

Serve the slices with a dollop of the stewed tomatoes on the side and garnish with a few thyme leaves.

Tip
I like the chewy saltiness of halloumi, but you could use Parmesan or other hard cheeses instead.

Teriyaki salmon steamed buns

Serves	Preparation time:	Resting time:	Cooking time:
4	20 minutes	1 hour 15 minutes	20 minutes

As a kid, getting hold of a savoury Asian bun in the suburbs of London or the Bavarian countryside was like trying to find Wi-Fi in the Sahara, so my brother and mum resorted to some DIY. Unfortunately the result wasn't a great success and the recipe wasn't repeated. Buns were saved for when we went to Chinatown as a special treat and could chow down on a basketful. It was only years later, when I came back to London and discovered a plethora of food trucks, bun-only restaurants and even buns on gastropub menus, that I decided it was time to have another bash at making some at home. I can assure you that you won't be needing a trip to London after you've made these.

2 tbsp light soy sauce or tamari

2 tbsp mirin

2 tbsp runny honey

I red chilli, cut into rounds

2 salmon fillets (approx. 150g each)

For the bun dough

160g plain flour, plus extra for dusting

1 tbsp dried skimmed milk powder

1½ tbsp caster sugar

1 scant tsp fast-action yeast

1 tsp baking powder

a pinch of sea salt

90ml warm water

1 tbsp vegetable oil, plus extra to grease and brush

To serve

a handful of fresh coriander leaves

1 lime, quartered

1 small cucumber, cut into thin rounds

4 spring onions, sliced thinly at an angle

Whisk together the soy, mirin, honey and chilli in a shallow baking dish, then add the salmon fillets, turning them to coat. Cover and place in the fridge.

Put the dry ingredients for the bun dough into a large bowl. Mix together, then make a well in the centre and add the wet ingredients. Use a spoon to bring together, then turn out and knead for 2–3 minutes, or until you have a smooth dough. Place in a bowl greased with vegetable oil and cover with a tea towel or a piece of cling film. Leave to rise for 45 minutes, or until nearly doubled in size.

Cut out 8 pieces of baking paper about 10cm x 10cm. Dust the work surface and your hands with flour. Roll the dough into a fat sausage and cut it into 8 equal parts. Roll each part into a ball, then dust your work surface again, flatten the ball and roll out with a rolling pin into a 15cm x 7cm oval shape about 3mm thick. Brush lightly with oil and fold in half. Place each on a square of baking paper and leave for 30 minutes to rise.

In the meantime, preheat the oven to 200°C (fan). Place the salmon in the oven and cook for 20 minutes, spooning the marinade over the fish about 10 minutes into the cooking time.

Set up a steamer and place the bun dough on the baking paper directly into it. Do this in batches if you don't have lots of space for them all, as they expand as they cook. Steam for 5–8 minutes, or until fluffy, pale and firm to the touch.

While you are steaming the buns, place the coriander, lime, cucumber and spring onions in separate bowls. When the salmon is cooked, pour any remaining marinade into a small jug. Serve the steamed buns with the teriyaki salmon, the bowls of garnishes and the sauce on the side for self-assembly.

Wholemeal open lasagna with creamy spinach and poached egg

Serves	Preparation time:	Resting time:	Cooking time:
4 as a light dinner or lunch	10 minutes	30 minutes	15–20 minutes

Normally I'm not one to make my own pasta, despite having bought a pasta machine many years ago on my first trip to Naples (which was so heavy I ended up paying extra baggage fees). Getting the machine out and having to deal with all the cleaning afterwards has always put me off. However, as I discovered when I was testing this recipe, making your own pasta doesn't have to be hard or time-consuming. And don't be put off by the idea of the wholemeal flour. It's not traditional, but it works particularly well with the robust flavour of the spinach.

500g frozen spinach

salt and freshly ground pepper

2 tbsp crème fraîche

4 eggs

50g grated Parmesan cheese or other flavoursome hard cheese, to serve

For the pasta dough

100g wholemeal flour, plus extra to dust

½ tsp sea salt

½ tsp freshly grated nutmeg

1 egg

1 tbsp water

Mix together the flour, salt and the nutmeg in a large bowl. Crack in 1 egg and add the water. Bring together with a spoon, then turn out on to a floured work surface and knead into a smooth ball. Wrap in cling film and leave to chill in the fridge for 30 minutes.

Place the frozen spinach in a medium saucepan. Cover and cook on a medium heat for 5 minutes, then uncover. Cook for another 10 minutes, until all the excess liquid has evaporated, stirring occasionally. Taste and season generously with salt and pepper, then stir in the crème fraîche.

Meanwhile, dust your work surface with flour, cut the dough into 4 parts and roll each with a rolling pin into a very thin pasta rectangle (about 20cm x 14cm and 1mm thick).

Bring a medium saucepan of salted water to a gentle simmer and a large saucepan of salted water to the boil. Crack 1 egg into a ramekin or glass (I find this makes it easiest to guide them into the water), then stir the water in the medium pan, making a little whirlpool, and pour the egg into the centre. Repeat with the rest of the eggs and leave to cook for 2–3 minutes. Use a slotted spoon to remove the eggs from the water and drain on a clean tea towel or kitchen towel. You can cut off any stray bits of white if you want to tidy them up.

Plunge the pasta sheets into the large pan of boiling water for 2–3 minutes, then remove with a slotted spoon and divide between 4 shallow bowls. Add a dollop of the spinach, follow with an egg, then fold the top of the sheet back over to encase the egg. Sprinkle with plenty of Parmesan cheese.

Cherry—glazed lamb shanks with pilaf

Serves	Preparation time:	Cooking time:
4	20 minutes	3 hours

Shanks seem to be the choice cut of lamb in gastropubs and restaurants. More affordable than shoulder, perfect for slow cooking, they require minimum effort for maximum flavour. Lamb can be a bit of a flavour bully, dominating a dish, so you need some distinct flavours to stand up to it. The cherries and red wine in this dish form fruity notes that really mellow out the lamb. There's not much to making it: browning the meat, popping the ingredients in and letting the magic happen in the pot.

3 tbsp plain flour

1 tsp each sea salt and freshly ground pepper

4 lamb shanks, 350–400g each

1–2 tbsp olive oil

400ml red wine such as Pinot Noir or Beaujolais

600ml chicken stock

2 x 440g tins of stoneless cherries, drained

300g basmati rice

50g butter

1 onion, peeled and finely chopped

50g pistachios, roughly chopped

2 sticks of celery, finely chopped

1 large carrot (200g), peeled and finely chopped

2 tsp cornflour

2 tbsp water

a handful of finely chopped fresh parsley

zest of 1 unwaxed lemon

Preheat the oven to 160°C (fan). Mix the flour, salt and pepper in a large bowl and add the lamb shanks, dusting each one well in the flour. Pour the oil into a large lidded ovenproof casserole pan over a medium heat and brown the shanks in batches. Pour in the wine, stock, and one of the tins of cherries. Bring everything up to the boil, cover and put in the oven for 2 hours, or until the meat feels very tender when poked with a knife. Remove the lid and cook for a further 30 minutes.

Twenty-five minutes before the lamb is ready, start to make the pilaf. Rinse the rice in water, drain, then repeat 3 times. Cook the rice in a large pan of boiling salted water for 5 minutes and drain well. Meanwhile, put the butter into a large lidded non-stick frying pan on a medium–low heat. Add the onion, pistachios, celery and carrot and fry gently for 10–15 minutes, or until they soften, then stir in the par-cooked rice and season with salt. Wrap the lid of the pan in a clean tea towel and place on top (the tea towel will absorb moisture so the rice stays crispy). Cook for 25 minutes on a very low heat – you want the rice to crisp up on the base of the pan.

Put the cornflour and water into a small bowl and mix to a smooth paste. Remove the lamb shanks to a plate and wrap in foil to keep warm. Pour the sauce through a sieve into a jug to remove the cherries (reserving them for later). Pour the sauce into a large pan, then skim off the fat with a large spoon and whisk in the diluted cornflour. Bring to a simmer and continue whisking for 10–15 minutes, or until the sauce coats the back of the spoon and becomes glossy. Season with plenty of pepper, and salt if needed. Put the cherries back into the sauce, along with the second tin of cherries, and warm through.

To serve, fluff up the pilaf with a fork and toss in the parsley and lemon zest. Divide between plates, place a shank on each plate and pour over some cherry sauce and cherries.

Pistachio and pomegranate cake

Sweets

Chocolate fancies

Shake and make ice cream

I've always had a keen interest in getting to the roots of an idea. To discover that the word 'dessert' originates from the French was no surprise, but its etymology was not what I expected. Its linguistic roots come from the mid-sixteenth-century word *desservir*, which means 'to clear away a table'. Back in medieval times, both savoury and sweet dishes would share the table simultaneously, and the serving of a dessert at the end of the meal was not de rigueur until a couple of centuries later. However, I can't think of a better way of finishing a meal than on a sweet note, leaving your guests on a sugar high.

Desserts are in my blood. From my fond childhood memories of licking cake batter off spoons, making gingerbread with my mum, or sitting at my Austrian grandma's table and watching her stretch out strudel dough, to my perfecting a buttery *pain au chocolat* in Paris, I feel at home when I'm whisking, folding, whipping or piping. There's something very soothing and satisfying about delicately smoothing icing on to a cake with strokes of your spatula, or placing that last cherry on to a dessert to complete a dish. The skill and craftsmanship are what initially drew me to study patisserie in Paris; unlike other sorts of cooking, there is a certain scientific precision to desserts. Too much butter and the batter spreads; too hot and the cake cracks – but don't let that put you off. It's very reassuring to know that if you weigh your ingredients and follow the method in the recipe, all will go well. And then there's the great pleasure in bringing the dessert to life with the decoration – like the marbling on my pistachio, yoghurt and pomegranate cake (page 163), or the Jackson Pollack-esque chocolate 'dribble' on my chocolate and courgette fondant fancies (page 196).

But it's not just about the eye candy, it has to taste good too! Whether it's combining classic flavours like cherry and chocolate in the Black Forest gâteau bowls (page 179); or unusual ones like those in my mini orange trifles with candied carrots (page 160) or different textures, such as the crunch and creamy elements in the edible forest floor (page 159), the recipes in this chapter will surprise, excite and tickle your taste buds.

Berry tartlets with cream cheese frosting

Makes	Preparation time:	Baking time:	Cooling time:
6	30 minutes	35 minutes	20 minutes

These delightful tartlets are easy to make, and look impressive with a little bouquet of fresh berries perched on top.

2–3 tbsp caster sugar

175g puff pastry

150–200g fresh berries (strawberries, raspberries, blueberries), washed

optional: icing sugar

For the cream cheese frosting

90g soft unsalted butter

125g icing sugar

90g full-fat cream cheese (removed from the fridge 30 minutes before using)

Equipment

a non-stick 6-hole muffin tin

Preheat the oven to 180°C (fan).

Dust the work surface with half the caster sugar and roll out the pastry in a landscape rectangle, roughly 15cm x 20cm. Dust with the remaining sugar and roll the rolling pin over it to press the sugar in. Tightly roll it up, starting from the horizontal side closest to you. Cut the roll into 6 equal-sized pieces, roughly 3cm wide. Take one piece and place it spiral side up in the muffin tin. Use your thumb to push the dough outwards, evenly lining the base and sides of the tin. Repeat with the rest of the spirals.

Prick the base of each one with a fork, then line with small rounds of baking paper and add ceramic baking beans to each. Bake for 20 minutes, then remove the beans and baking paper and return to the oven for a further 10–15 minutes, or until lightly golden and cooked through (check by lifting one out of the tin). Remove from the tin immediately (otherwise they will caramelize and stick), and leave to cool on a wire rack before decorating.

Using an electric hand whisk, beat together the butter and icing sugar for 2 minutes, or until light and fluffy. Beat in the cream cheese until well blended.

To assemble, dollop the frosting on to each of the tartlet bases. Decorate the tops with berries, and dust with icing sugar if you like.

Get ahead

Once cooled, the baked tartlet bases can be kept in an airtight container for 5 days. They also freeze well.

Tip
Don't refrigerate the ganache or the chocolate yoghurt as they will become too hard to use.

Get ahead
The meringue mushrooms without ganache will keep for about a week in an airtight container.

Edible forest floor

Serves 4	Preparation time: 30 minutes	Cooking time: 1½–2 hours	Cooling time: 2 hours minimum

The Swedish forest inspires this dessert. I've spent many summers in Sweden picking berries. Plated desserts are a common sight on restaurant menus and can look intimidating to the home cook, but it's simply a case of bringing together different tastes, textures and sometimes temperatures to work in harmony. Here you get crunch from the meringue, richness from the ganache, creaminess from the yoghurt and tartness from the berries. It's the combination of these elements that makes the dessert work.

100g Bourbon or other chocolate biscuits

100g blueberries or berries of your choice

fresh mint leaves

For the meringue mushrooms

35g egg white (from 1 medium egg)

a pinch of sea salt

50g caster sugar

1 tbsp cocoa powder

For the dark chocolate ganache

100g dark chocolate (70%), broken into pieces

100ml double cream

a pinch of sea salt

For the milk chocolate yoghurt

160g milk chocolate, broken into pieces

200g natural full-fat yoghurt

Equipment

piping bags with 1cm and 3–4mm nozzles

a chopstick

Preheat the oven to 100°C (fan). To make the meringue mushrooms, put the egg white and salt into a large glass bowl and whisk with an electric hand whisk or use a standing mixer. When really frothy, gradually add the sugar, whisking until the meringue is thick and glossy and forms stiff, shiny peaks.

Line an oven tray with baking paper. Spoon the meringue into a piping bag fitted with a 1cm nozzle, and squeeze out into 12 round mounds, 2–3cm wide, to make the mushroom caps. To make each stem, separately squeeze out a bit of meringue on to the tray, then pull the bag straight up so each one stands 3–4cm high. Dip your finger in water and smooth the top of the mushroom caps so that they're rounded. Bake in the centre of the oven for 1½ hours, then turn the oven off. Don't peek. Leave them for 2 hours or overnight until completely cool and dried out.

To make the dark chocolate ganache, place the chocolate in a heatproof bowl. Put the cream and salt into a small saucepan and bring to a simmer, then pour over the chocolate. Leave to sit for 2 minutes, then stir until thoroughly incorporated. Leave to cool for about 30 minutes, or until room temperature, then spoon into a piping bag with a 3–4mm nozzle.

To assemble the mushrooms, use a chopstick to make a small hole in the underside of each mushroom cap. Pipe a small amount of chocolate ganache into each hole, then stick the stems in. Dust with a tiny amount of cocoa powder.

For the milk chocolate yoghurt, place the chocolate and yoghurt in a heatproof bowl over a pan of just-simmering water (don't let the bowl touch the water). Stir until the chocolate has dissolved, using a whisk to mix well.

To assemble, spread a layer of chocolate yoghurt on to each dessert plate. Crumble over the Bourbon biscuits, and pipe dots of the dark chocolate ganache on randomly. Stick a few mushrooms on top, then dot over the berries and mint leaves.

Mini orange trifles with candied carrot

Serves	Preparation time:	Cooking time:	Chilling time:
4	30 minutes	15 minutes	4 hours minimum

This recipe takes its inspiration from the classic Provençal dish *petits farcis*, in which Mediterranean vegetables are stuffed with rice or mince. I decided to go a bit retro, filling oranges with jelly, but adding candied carrots and snow-white meringue to transform a children's classic into something a bit more modern.

For the candied carrots

150g caster sugar

150ml water

1 large carrot (100g), peeled and julienned (use a mandolin)

For the orange jelly

2 large oranges

2 leaves of gelatin

For the meringue topping

2 egg whites

110g caster sugar

Equipment

a piping bag

a blow torch (optional)

Place the sugar, water and julienned carrot in a large saucepan over a gentle heat. Bring to the boil, stirring occasionally until the sugar has melted, then simmer briskly for around 10 minutes until the carrot looks shiny. Remove from the heat and drain in a sieve set over a bowl.

Halve the oranges and juice them carefully (you want to maintain their shape as they will act as the jelly containers). Strain the juice through a sieve and set aside. Use a teaspoon to scoop the inside membrane out of the orange halves, until you are left with just a thin layer of pith and the skin. Take a little slice out of the base of each orange half so that they sit upright.

Soak the gelatin in a bowl of cold water for 5 minutes. Mix the carrot syrup with the squeezed orange juice. Place in a small saucepan and heat very gently until warm, then squeeze out the soaked gelatin sheets and stir them into the liquid. Keep stirring until dissolved, then pour into a jug.

Mould some aluminium foil around the bases of the oranges to help make them sit straight. Place on a tray and take them to the fridge with the jelly. Pour the jelly into the moulds while they're on the fridge shelf.

Divide some of the candied carrots between the orange halves. Leave to set in the fridge for at least 4 hours or overnight.

When you are ready to serve, preheat the oven to 180°C (fan).

To make the meringue topping, spread the sugar out on a baking tray and place in the oven for about 10 minutes. Whisk the egg whites until frothy and add the hot sugar one spoonful at a time. Continue to whisk until cool and glossy. Place the meringue in a piping bag. Pipe a large dollop of meringue on top of each jelly.

If you like, use a blow torch to lightly toast the tips of the meringue. Decorate with a few strips of the candied carrot, and serve.

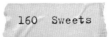

Tip

Use any leftover candied carrot to decorate a carrot cake. They keep well in the fridge for a few days.

Get ahead

The jelly will keep in the fridge for a couple of days, but make the meringue just before serving.

Pistachio and pomegranate cake

Serves 8-10	Preparation time: 20 minutes	Baking time: 50 minutes

Turkish pastries, such as the intensely sweet and extremely sticky baklava, were nothing new to me; however, the pomegranate juice stands that cropped up on Istanbul's street corners were a delightful discovery. The dark red juice makes for a refreshing drink, and although it's a nightmare if you get it on your clothes, it's perfect for colouring icing the natural way.

For the sponge

2 x 150g pots of natural yoghurt

100g pistachio kernels

1 x 150g yoghurt pot of caster sugar

1 x 150g yoghurt pot of sunflower oil

2 eggs, lightly beaten

1 tsp vanilla extract

2 x 150g yoghurt pots of plain flour

2 tsp baking powder

½ tsp sea salt

For the yoghurt icing

½ a pomegranate

250g icing sugar

50g natural yoghurt

Equipment

a 20cm springform tin, buttered and floured

Preheat the oven to 160°C (fan).

Empty the contents of the yoghurt pots into a bowl, then wash and dry them ready to measure the remaining ingredients. You'll need one for wet ingredients and one for dry ingredients. Whizz the pistachios to a fine powder in a blender.

Put the caster sugar and oil in a large bowl or standing mixer bowl, then mix together with an electric hand whisk or the whisk attachment for 2 minutes, until the sugar has dissolved. Gradually add the eggs and vanilla extract. Fold in the yoghurt, then add the flour, baking powder, salt and ground pistachios and gently fold them in.

Spoon the batter into the tin. Bake for 50 minutes or until a skewer comes out clean. Leave to cool for 5 minutes before turning out on to a wire rack to cool.

When the cake is cool, place the pomegranate skin side up in your hand with your fingers spread out. Hold the pomegranate just inside a big bowl before hitting the back of the fruit with a wooden spoon. The seeds will fall through the gaps between your fingers.

Sift the icing sugar into a bowl, then add the yoghurt and mix well to get a thick pouring consistency. Pour on top of the cooled cake, gently guiding it down the sides. Once the icing has stopped dripping, take the pomegranate juice and dot several drops along the top of the cake. Drag a skewer or toothpick in a figure-of-eight pattern through the drips of pomegranate, swirling it all around the cake.

Stick the pomegranate seeds to the side of the cake when the icing has stopped dripping. If it's difficult to make them stick, chill the cake for 10 minutes in the fridge first.

Underground éclairs

Makes	Preparation time:	Cooking time:	Cooling time:
8	35 minutes	25–30 minutes	1 hour

These tubes of choux pastry are my ode to London's almighty Tube. Instead of opting for artificial food colourings, I've picked some fresh fruits that correspond with the colours of some of my favourite Underground lines. Well, no one actually likes the District line, let's be honest, but kiwis accessorize these éclairs beautifully.

65ml water

65ml whole milk

50g unsalted butter, cubed

½ teaspoon sea salt

½ teaspoon caster sugar

85g strong plain flour

2 eggs

For the pastry cream

3 egg yolks

40g caster sugar

20g cornflour

250ml whole milk

1 vanilla pod

For the icing

100g fondant or royal icing sugar, sifted

½ an egg white

¾ – 1 tsp lemon juice

Preheat the oven to 180°C (fan).

Pour the water and milk into a medium saucepan and add the butter, salt and sugar. Place the pan on a high heat and melt the butter. Bring to the boil, then turn the heat down to low and add the flour. Beat hard. At this point the mixture will have the consistency of lumpy mashed potatoes. Continue beating for about 1 minute, until you have a smooth ball that pulls away from the sides of the pan without sticking.

Take the pan off the heat and continue to beat for about 4–5 minutes, or until the dough is cold enough to touch. Mix in the eggs one at a time – the batter will go lumpy when you add them, but beating continuously will smooth it out. Once both eggs are incorporated and the mixture is smooth, put the dough into a piping bag with a 20mm plain nozzle.

Line a large baking tray with baking paper, dotting a little dough in each corner to stick the paper down. Pipe a 10cm line of the choux mixture at a 45-degree angle. Repeat with the remaining dough to make 8 éclairs. Bake for 25 minutes, or until golden and crisp, and leave to cool on a wire rack.

While the éclairs are baking, make the pastry cream. Put the egg yolks and sugar into a large bowl and whisk until light and fluffy with an electric hand whisk, or use a standing mixer, then whisk in the cornflour. Pour the milk into a saucepan. Split the vanilla pod lengthways, scrape out the seeds and add to the milk. Bring the milk to scalding point, then switch off the heat.

Pour the milk in a slow stream on to the egg mixture, whisking vigorously. Return the mixture to a clean saucepan and whisk continuously over a medium heat. Make sure you scrape the sides and the bottom, otherwise it will burn. The cream will start

For the fruits

Central line: 5 small strawberries, hulled

District line: 1 kiwi fruit, peeled

Circle line: 40g slice of pineapple, peeled

Hammersmith & City: 50g raspberries

Equipment

a piping bag with a 20mm plain nozzle

to thicken. Once it releases a bubble or two, take it off the heat. Pour into a bowl and place cling film directly on the cream so that it doesn't form a skin. Leave to cool to room temperature, then refrigerate for at least an hour before using.

When ready to use, beat the cream to smooth it out and place in a piping or food bag. Cut the éclairs open horizontally and pipe pastry cream inside, then put the top back on and make the icing.

Mix the icing sugar with the egg white and lemon juice until you have a very thick paste. If it's too runny it won't stick to the fruits properly, in which case just add a little more icing sugar.

Slice the strawberries, kiwi fruit and pineapple thinly. Spread a thin line of icing along the top of each éclair lid. Decorate 2 éclairs with the strawberries, lining them up along the top of the pastry and using the icing to stick them down. Then decorate the rest of the éclairs with the kiwi fruits, pineapple and raspberries respectively.

Spiced apple tray cake

Serves	Preparation time:	Cooking time:
14	20 minutes	50–60 minutes

There's nothing more homely than the smell of cinnamon and baking apples. This would be the perfect cake to bake if you were trying to sell your home.

I had an amazing slice of apple cake when I was in Amsterdam, where they pride themselves on it: buttery caramel pastry with a mix of both soft tender apple pieces and ones with bite (a combination of apples are a must). I've added roasted ground hazelnuts to my batter, which gives the finished product a deliciously nutty, almost frangipane flavour. The pastry is similar to one used in the Austrian cake my mum and aunts make, *Linzertorte* (hazelnut pastry with raspberry jam) – one of my favourites.

200g blanched hazelnuts or almonds

360g soft unsalted butter

225g soft light brown sugar

a good pinch of sea salt

3 medium eggs, lightly beaten

400g plain flour

4 tsp baking powder

optional: 1 tbsp icing sugar, to serve

For the filling

30g soft light brown sugar (plus extra for the topping)

1 tbsp ground cinnamon

½ tsp ground ginger

¼ tsp grated nutmeg

2 tbsp cornflour

3 firm apples (such as Braeburn, Royal Gala, Cox)

5 medium Bramley cooking apples

Equipment

a 30cm square cake tin, buttered

a piping or food bag

Preheat the oven to 160°C (fan).

Put the nuts into a dry pan on a medium heat. Toast for about 5 minutes, or until the nuts are golden, stirring frequently. Remove from the pan and let the nuts cool completely, then blend them in a food processor to a fine powder.

Cream together the butter, soft light brown sugar and salt in a large bowl. Mix in the eggs gradually. In a separate bowl mix together the flour, baking powder and ground nuts, then fold gently into the butter mix.

Spread two-thirds of the batter across the base of the cake tin. Keep the base even, but scrape it up a little at the sides to create an edge to hold the filling.

To make the filling, mix the soft light brown sugar, spices and cornflour in a large bowl. Peel, core and cut the apples into 2cm cubes, then toss well in the spice mix. Scatter the filling over the cake batter and level out evenly.

Place the remaining cake batter in a piping bag or food bag with the end snipped off, and pipe 4 lines of batter one way over the top of the cake, then 4 lines the other way, to make a lattice pattern. Bake for 50–60 minutes, or until the crust is golden brown.

Leave to cool for 10 minutes, then remove from the tin and dust with icing sugar (if using). Serving warm with a dollop of whipped cream or a scoop of vanilla ice cream.

Tip

If you can't find blanched hazelnuts, roast unblanched ones for 8–10 minutes at 120°C (fan) and rub the skins off with a clean tea towel.

Raspberry and grape brioche and butter pudding

Serves
4

Preparation time:
20 minutes

Baking time:
15 minutes

In the sweet department, France is best known for its extravagant patisseries. However, when you head out to the countryside, heartier portions and rustic-looking cakes are more the norm. This is where the French grand-mère is the queen of the kitchen, not some Parisian chef with lots of airs and graces.

Bread and butter pudding isn't exactly on the menu in France, but the brioche, fruity compote and crème anglaise give this British classic a fantastic French twist. This is also a great way to give old brioche a whole new lease of life.

80g caster sugar

300g frozen raspberries

4 tbsp Chambord, or other raspberry-flavoured liqueur

300g dark red grapes (ideally muscat), cut in half, seeds removed

8 x 1.5cm-thick slices of brioche, ideally a few days old

2 knobs of soft unsalted butter

For the crème anglaise

250ml whole milk

250ml double cream

1 vanilla pod

4 egg yolks

50g caster sugar

Place 30g of sugar, the frozen raspberries and Chambord in a medium saucepan over a low heat. Cover with a lid and cook for about 6 minutes, or until the raspberries have softened, stirring occasionally. Take off the heat and stir in the grape halves, then cover the pan and set aside.

Meanwhile, make the crème anglaise. Pour the milk and cream into a medium saucepan. Split the vanilla pod in half lengthways and scrape out the seeds into the pan, adding the pod too. Bring to a simmer over a medium-low heat. In a large separate bowl, whisk the egg yolks with the sugar. Pour a little of the hot cream mixture on to the yolks, whisking vigorously, then gradually pour in the rest of the liquid. Remove the vanilla pod and return the mixture to a clean pan.

On a medium-low heat, whisk the cream and egg mixture continuously until it thickens to the consistency of double cream; don't let it come near boiling point or it might split. As soon as it has thickened, pour straight into a jug or bowl and cover the surface with cling film to prevent a skin forming. Set aside until ready to use.

To prepare the brioche slices, preheat the grill to medium. Spread 50g of sugar on to a large plate. If the brioche is fresh, simply dip in the sugar; otherwise spread butter on both sides before pressing in the sugar. Place under the grill on a baking tray lined with foil, turning over after a couple of minutes or when the brioche is golden. (Beware, it can brown very quickly.)

Before assembling the pudding, reheat the grape and raspberry compote and the crème anglaise. Place a slice of brioche in 4 shallow bowls. Pour on a few tablespoons of the hot compote, followed by another slice of brioche. Ladle over the warm crème anglaise, followed by several more spoons of the compote, and serve immediately.

Plum jelly with elderflower chantilly

| Serves 12 | Preparation time: 30 minutes | Cooking time: 20 minutes | Resting time: 12 hours minimum |

I love the wibble-wobble of jelly on a plate. The texture is immensely satisfying when paired with lashings of Chantilly cream, proving that jelly isn't just fun for kids.

For the plum jelly
2kg purple or red plums
750ml water
650g caster sugar
12 gelatin leaves

For the crystallized basil leaves
1 egg white
4–6 tbsp caster sugar
a handful of basil leaves

For the Chantilly cream
525ml whipping cream
75g caster sugar
3 tbsp elderflower cordial

Equipment
a 1.5 litre jelly mould, lightly oiled

Halve the plums, leaving the stones in, and place in a large saucepan with the water and sugar over a medium heat. Bring to a simmer, stirring frequently to help dissolve the sugar, then lower the heat. Simmer the plums uncovered for 15–20 minutes, or until mushy.

Half fill a large wide container with cold water, then add the gelatin leaves one at a time, so they don't stick together. Leave to soak for 10 minutes.

Drain the plums in a colander set over a large jug or bowl, reserving the syrup. Then pass the plums through a fine sieve into the jug or bowl, pressing out as much of the plum juice as you can. Discard the stones, but keep the stewed fruit for another day (see tips).

Squeeze the water from the soaked gelatin leaves and add to the plum syrup. Stir until dissolved, then pour into your jelly mould. Dab with kitchen towel if there is any scum at the top. Leave to cool completely, then cover and put in the fridge for at least 12 hours or overnight.

When the jelly has set, crystallize the basil leaves. Place the egg white in a bowl and whisk lightly to loosen. Place the sugar on a plate, and have a clean plate to hand. Dip a clean paintbrush or pastry brush into the egg white and delicately coat a basil leaf. Sprinkle the leaf with sugar, then place on the clean plate. Repeat with the remaining leaves and set aside in a cool, dark place.

Before serving, whip the cream with the sugar until it forms soft peaks, then fold in the elderflower cordial. Remove the jelly from its mould and place on a cake stand. Dollop the Chantilly cream around the edge of the jelly and arrange the basil leaves on top.

Tips
The leftover stewed fruit goes well with yoghurt and granola.
To remove the jelly from the mould, dip the mould quickly in hot water.
Use the basil leaves within 1–2 hours of serving as they tend to lose their vibrant colour.

Honey-roasted peach crema catalana

Makes	Preparation time:	Cooking time:	Standing time:
4	20 minutes	45 minutes	30 minutes infusing, plus 2 hours chilling

One of the best parts of a *crema catalana* is breaking through the caramel crust and diving into the rich, smooth cream, but I often find it overbearingly sweet. So here I have swapped the caramel topping for peaches (nectarines or apricots would work too), which I spotted in all the markets when I visited the Costa Brava. Placed on top of the creams, the juicy, honey-roasted peaches create a delicious fruity crust.

Vanilla pod is normally used to flavour the cream, but I like to use the kernels from the peaches, which add a subtle almond flavour. It can be a pain to crack them open though, so if you want to cheat and use a splash of almond essence, I will forgive you.

2 ripe peaches

3 tbsp runny honey

500ml whole milk

4 egg yolks

60g caster sugar

2 tbsp cornflour

Equipment

4 x 120ml ramekins

a hammer or nutcracker

Preheat the oven to 160°C (fan). Cut the peaches in half and remove the stones. Place the peaches cut side up on a baking tray and drizzle with the honey. Cover with baking paper and roast in the oven for 30 minutes, or until tender but not mushy.

Meanwhile, use a hammer or nutcracker to crack open the peach stones and remove the peach kernels. If using a hammer, place each stone in a clean tea towel, then fold the cloth over the top to secure the stone, before bashing it. Place the kernels in a saucepan and add the milk. Slowly bring to scalding point, then remove from the heat. Leave to infuse for 30 minutes.

In a large bowl, whisk the egg yolks with the sugar for 2–3 minutes until pale, then add the cornflour. Slowly whisk in the cooled milk. Pour the custard back into a clean pan and place over a gentle heat, whisking continuously for 8–10 minutes, or until the mixture has thickened and releases a bubble or two.

Remove and discard the kernels, and divide the mixture between the 4 ramekins. Peel the skin off the peach halves and place one half cut side down on top of each ramekin. Leave to cool for 30 minutes, or until room temperature, then place in the fridge and leave to set for at least 2 hours before serving.

Tip
Crack your peach stones gently, so as not to break the kernels.

Black forest gâteau bowls

Makes
8 cups

Preparation time:
45 minutes

Resting time:
30 minutes

Cooking time:
30–35 minutes

This recipe combines all the classic ingredients of the great retro Black Forest gâteau. For an impressive, dainty twist, try serving it in these cute homemade chocolate cups.

For the sponge

90g plain flour

2 tbsp cocoa powder

1 tsp baking powder

125g caster sugar

2 eggs

50g unsalted butter, melted

For the chocolate bowls

400g dark chocolate (70%), broken into pieces

2 tbsp vegetable or sunflower oil, plus extra to grease

For the cherries

400g cherries

100ml water

100g caster sugar

To decorate

300ml whipping cream

1 tbsp icing sugar, sifted

Equipment

a 20cm round cake tin, buttered and floured

8 small balloons

a piping bag

Preheat the oven to 160°C (fan). To make the sponge, sift together the flour, cocoa powder and baking powder in a bowl. In a separate large bowl or standing mixer, whisk the caster sugar and eggs for 7–8 minutes, or until pale and fluffy. Add the melted butter and fold into the eggs, followed by the sifted flour mixture.

Pour into the cake tin. Bake for 30–35 minutes, or until a skewer comes out clean. Remove from the tin after 5 minutes and leave on a wire rack to cool.

Meanwhile, blow up the balloons until roughly 10cm in diameter, then tie them. Put the broken chocolate into a small heatproof bowl with the oil and place over a small pan of just-simmering water (don't let the bowl touch the water). Leave to melt, stirring occasionally, then set aside for 10–15 minutes. As it stands it will thicken; you want it to be the consistency of double cream. Cover a plate with some lightly oiled cling film, then dip your balloon into the chocolate and place on the plate. Put into the fridge to set.

Pit the cherries (putting aside 8 whole ones with stems for the garnish). Pour the water and 100g caster sugar into a medium saucepan over a medium heat and bring to a simmer. Add the cherries and cook gently for 10 minutes, then remove from the heat and leave to cool to room temperature. Place in the fridge to chill.

Once the first layer of chocolate has set, repeat with a second layer. (You will probably need to reheat the chocolate in the bain-marie or microwave for a couple of seconds.) Return to the fridge. Once set, the balloons can be removed. Simply snip the across the top of them and let the air out, then gently pull them away to reveal the bowls.

Cut the cake into small chunks and divide between the bowls. Top with the cherries, drizzling over some of the syrup. Whisk the cream with the icing sugar until it forms soft peaks and place in a piping bag. Pipe a swirl of cream on top of each bowl, followed by a reserved whole cherry.

Tips

Don't dip the balloons into very hot chocolate, as they will explode and make a big mess. It's also better to dip them into a small bowl of chocolate to give the chocolate layer more depth.

It's easier to whip cream when the cream is really cold. If it's hot in your kitchen, place your bowl in the freezer before you whip. You can use a thick plastic straw to pit cherries if you don't have a cherry pitter.

Lemon lava cakes

Makes	Preparation time:	Cooking time:	Cooling time:
6	25 minutes	30 minutes	20–30 minutes

What do you get when you cross an Amalfi lemon, Vesuvius and a cake? A lemon lava cake! OK, I know my joke is appalling, but that's how I got the idea for this recipe. The Amalfi coast is blessed with an abundance of citrus fruits, which line the coastal roads that cling to the cliffs. This little cake erupts like the nearby Mount Vesuvius, with a zingy hot lemon curd. It's dessert with attitude: a punchy lemon flavour and an exploding centre.

For the lemon curd

juice of 3 lemons (approx. 110ml)

200g caster sugar

2 eggs

a pinch of sea salt

50g cold unsalted butter, cubed

For the sponge

100g soft unsalted butter, plus extra to grease ramekins

80g caster sugar, plus 1 tbsp to dust ramekins

2 eggs

2 tbsp whole milk

zest of 3 unwaxed lemons

100g plain flour

Equipment

a disposable piping or food bag

6 x 120ml ramekins

Place all the ingredients for the lemon curd, apart from the butter, in a medium saucepan on a gentle heat and whisk continuously for 5–8 minutes, or until the mixture thickens. Whisk in the butter, cube by cube. Take off the heat once all the butter has dissolved. Pour into a wide bowl and cool for around 20–30 minutes, or until room temperature. Pour into a disposable piping bag or a heavy-duty food bag, and refrigerate until using.

Preheat the oven to 180°C (fan). Butter the ramekins and dust with sugar.

To make the sponge, beat the butter and sugar until fluffy. Lightly beat the eggs and gradually add them to the mix, beating all the time, followed by the milk and lemon zest. Sift the flour into the mix and incorporate well. Divide the cake batter between the ramekins until just over half full.

Take the piping or food bag and snip off the corner. Insert the tip into the centre of each batter-filled ramekin. Pipe the curd into each one until the ramekins are two-thirds full. Place on a baking tray.

Bake for 15–20 minutes, or until the tops are golden and spring back when touched.

Immediately run a knife around the edges of the cakes before turning out from the ramekins on to plates. Serve straight away.

Tips
Make sure not to let the curd boil, as this will make it split and give it an eggy taste.

The leftover lemon curd is delicious swirled into yoghurt.

Get ahead
You can bake these from frozen. Simply fill the ramekins as per the recipe and place in the freezer. Preheat the oven to 170°C (fan) and cook for about 25 minutes.

BEAUTIFUL PASTRIES
SPOTTED IN ✖ A PÂTISSERIE

CRAZY CAKE DISPLAY IN A
RESTAURANT IN WARSAW ✖

CUTE COFFEE ART IN
STOCKHOLM

TESTING RHUBARB AND
CUSTARD MILLEFEUILLE
✖ RECIPE

LOADS OF SPOONS AT
THE GRAND BAZAAR
IN ✖ ISTANBUL

STRAWBERRY CREAM
CAKE ✖ YUM!

CHECKING OUT A NEW
PÂTISSERIE ✖ IN PARIS

COLOURFUL SELECTION
OF ICE LOLLIES
IN NEW ✖ YORK CITY

RHUBARB WITH
HOMEMADE SPICED JUNKET
✖

FRESH FRUIT

coconut
chocolate
coffee

JAM

SUGAR

COPPER
POT

Lingonberry and raspberry Mazarin tart

Serves
10

Preparation time:
25 minutes

Baking time:
55 minutes

Chilling time:
30 minutes minimum

Small versions of this tart can be found in almost every bakery across Sweden. Traditionally filled with a dense almond paste and encased in a buttery crust, they are perfect with a cup of coffee for what the Swedes call *fika* (coffee and cake time). My variation has some fruity extras, with a lingonberry jam base and raspberries on top: a Swedish-style Bakewell tart fit to grace any Parisian patisserie.

For the pastry
90g plain flour

a pinch of sea salt

1 tsp caster sugar

50g cold unsalted butter, cubed

1 egg yolk

1 tsp vodka, unflavoured schnapps or eau de vie

For the filling
150g blanched almonds

50g caster sugar

75g soft unsalted butter

½ tsp almond extract

a pinch of sea salt

2 eggs

1 tbsp plain flour

175g lingonberry jam

To decorate
100g icing sugar

1 tbsp water

200g raspberries

Equipment
a 20cm tart tin, buttered and floured

a piping or sandwich bag

Make the pastry by mixing the flour, salt and caster sugar together. Add the butter and rub together until you have a sandy texture. Combine the egg yolk and vodka and add to the mixture. Bring the mixture together, lightly kneading into a smooth dough. Try not to overwork it.

Roll the pastry out into a circular shape between two sheets of baking paper to 2mm thick. Line the tart tin and trim away any excess pastry, making sure the sides of the pastry are 2mm higher than the sides of the tin. Leave to rest in the fridge for at least 30 minutes or overnight.

Preheat the oven to 160°C (fan). Line the pastry with baking paper and fill with baking beans. Place the tart tin on a baking sheet and bake for 20 minutes, then remove the paper and beans and bake for a further 10 minutes. Remove from the oven and allow to cool.

Meanwhile, make the filling. Toast the blanched almonds in a dry frying pan for 3–4 minutes, or until golden, stirring constantly. Tip out on to a plate and leave to cool, then blitz with the caster sugar in a food processor until fine. Add the butter, almond extract and salt, and pulse to combine. Add the eggs and flour and pulse briefly again to combine.

Spread the jam on the base of the tart. Put the almond paste into a piping or a sandwich bag with the end snipped off, then pipe it in a spiral, starting from the centre and moving outwards. Place back in the oven to bake for another 20 minutes, or until the almond paste is firm and lightly golden. Leave to cool.

To decorate, mix the icing sugar with the water to make a very thick paste. Spread over the tart and arrange the raspberries on top.

Rhubarb and custard millefeuilles

Makes	Preparation time:	Cooking time:	Resting time:
4	40 minutes	35 minutes	1–2 hours

Rhubarb and custard, a classic combination I remember fondly from my childhood, when I would be given the hard-boiled flavoured sweets on long car journeys to keep me quiet. My dessert version has kept a few of my dinner guests quiet too.

1 x 375g pack of ready-rolled puff pastry (remove from fridge 20 minutes before using)

1 egg, beaten

2 tbsp caster sugar

1 tbsp icing sugar

For the custard

3 egg yolks

40g caster sugar

20g cornflour

250ml whole milk

½ a vanilla pod

For the rhubarb compote

400g pink forced rhubarb (approx. 8 sticks), washed, trimmed and cut into 10cm pieces

50g caster sugar

Equipment

a large piping bag with a 1cm nozzle

First make the custard. Whisk the egg yolks with the caster sugar for 2–3 minutes, or until light and thick, then whisk in the cornflour. Pour the milk into a saucepan, split the vanilla pod lengthways, scrape out the seeds and add to the milk, along with the pod. Bring the milk to the boil and turn off the heat. Pour the milk in a slow stream on to the egg mixture, whisking vigorously all the time.

Return the mixture to a clean saucepan and whisk continuously over a medium heat. Make sure you scrape the sides and the bottom, otherwise it will burn. The cream will start to thicken. Once it releases a bubble or two, take it off the heat. Pour the custard into a wide bowl to cool to room temperature. When it has cooled, spoon into a large piping bag with a 1cm nozzle and place in a jug so it stays upright. Put into the fridge to chill for 1–2 hours.

Preheat the oven to 180°C (fan). Line a baking tray with baking paper (or use the paper rolled around the puff pastry).

Cut the puff pastry into 12 rectangles measuring 4cm x 10cm and place on the baking tray. Brush lightly with the beaten egg and sprinkle with the caster sugar. Cover the glazed rectangles with baking paper, then place another baking tray on top; this will stop the pastry rising. Bake for 30 minutes.

Meanwhile, toss the rhubarb in the caster sugar and place in a small baking dish or roasting tray in the oven on a shelf under the pastry for 20 minutes. The rhubarb should be tender but not mushy.

To assemble, pipe 2 blobs of custard on to an individual serving plate. Stick a pastry rectangle on top, then place 3–4 rhubarb pieces on the pastry. Gently place another pastry rectangle over the rhubarb. Pipe 2 lines of custard on the second rectangle and top with a third rectangle. Repeat to make 4 millefeuilles. Dust with icing sugar and serve immediately.

Tip

If your pastry rectangles don't look quite done after 30 minutes, remove from the oven and take off the top baking tray and paper. Place the pastries back in the oven for a further 6–8 minutes.

Strawberry and cream layer cake

Makes
1 cake

Preparation time:
40 minutes

Cooking time:
45–50 minutes

Strawberries and cream are a match made in heaven. Combine that with the sound of Wimbledon on the TV and you pretty much have my memories of British summers.

For the spiced strawberries

800g strawberries, plus 100g to garnish

150ml water

150g caster sugar

a pinch of sea salt

1 tsp freshly ground black pepper

For the sponge

75g unsalted butter, melted

3 eggs

125g caster sugar

150g natural yoghurt

300g plain flour

1 tbsp baking powder

a pinch of sea salt

For the cream

1 vanilla pod, halved and seeds removed

750ml whipping cream

100g caster sugar

Equipment

a 19cm cake tin, lined with baking paper and buttered

Halve 800g of the strawberries. Place the water, sugar, salt and pepper in a medium saucepan and bring to a boil. Stir over a medium heat until the sugar has completely dissolved. Take off the heat, cool to room temperature, then chill in the fridge until needed.

Preheat the oven to 160°C (fan). Put the eggs and sugar into a large bowl or standing mixer bowl and whisk with an electric hand whisk or with the whisk attachment for about 5 minutes, or until thick, pale and fluffy. Pour in the melted butter and yoghurt.

Sift the flour, baking powder and salt into a separate bowl and mix well. Fold lightly into the egg mixture.

Bake for 45–50 minutes, or until a skewer comes out clean. Remove the tin from the oven for 5 minutes, then remove the cake from the tin and place on a wire rack.

Leave to cool for at least 30 minutes before slicing horizontally into 3. If you have a plate with a lip, you can do this by placing the whole cake upside down on the plate and using the edge of the plate to guide the bread knife across in a straight line, removing the peaked top (you can discard this). Repeat until you have 3 layers of cake.

Add the vanilla seeds to the cream and whip with the sugar until firm enough to ice the cake.

Pour the spiced strawberries into a sieve set over a bowl and leave to drain thoroughly.

Assemble the cake by using the top layer of sponge, inverted, as the base (that way the original flat base of the cake can be used as the top, giving a smooth finish). Use a pastry brush to dab the cut side of the cake generously with the syrup drained from the strawberries. Spread a quarter of the cream on top of the cake, then add half the macerated strawberries.

Place on another layer of sponge and repeat the process again. Finally spread or pipe the rest of the cream around the sides and on top of the cake. Top the cake with the remaining fresh strawberries. Serve immediately, or chill in the fridge for up to 2 days.

Tip

Dip your palette knife in hot water when icing to give a smoother finish.

Get ahead

The spiced strawberries can be made in advance. The sponge can be made a day in advance. Wrap well in cling film once cool.

Turkish coffee creams

Makes	Prep time:	Cooking time:	Resting time:	Chilling time:
6	30 minutes	15 minutes	30 minutes	4 hours

Coffee in Istanbul is not for the faint-hearted. It's deeply intense and bitter, with the remnants of coffee grains lying at the bottom of your cup. The grains can be used just like tea leaves to read your fortune. The syrup in the dessert gives the cream a serious coffee hit, just like the coffee I had in Istanbul. It's the ideal finale to a long meal.

For the coffee syrup
100g granulated sugar

100ml water

30ml espresso

For the coffee cream
100ml whole milk

150ml really strong coffee or espresso

a pinch of sea salt

3 egg yolks

80g caster sugar

1 heaped tbsp cornflour

100ml double cream

For the chocolate mendiants
100g dark chocolate (70%)

a pinch of sea salt

2 tbsp pistachios, roughly chopped

3 dried apricots, cut into thin strips

2 rose Turkish delights, chopped into small pieces

Equipment
6 small espresso cups, Turkish coffee cups or shot glasses

To make the syrup, put the granulated sugar and the water in a small pan over a low heat and bring to a simmer, swirling the pan. Simmer briskly for 5 minutes until thick and glossy. Add the shot of espresso and pour into a small bowl. Leave to cool for about 20 minutes, or until room temperature, then chill in the fridge for 1 hour.

To make the coffee cream, pour the milk and coffee into a pan over a medium heat, add the salt and bring it to scalding point. In the meantime, put the egg yolks and caster sugar into a bowl and whisk for 4–5 minutes, or until pale and fluffy, then fold in the cornflour.

Slowly pour the hot coffee mix over the egg mixture, whisking continuously. Return the mix to a clean saucepan and continue to whisk over a medium heat until the mixture releases a few bubbles and turns very thick and creamy. Take off the heat, pour into a bowl and put a piece of cling film directly on to the surface of the cream. Cool to room temperature, then place in the fridge to chill for 1 hour.

Meanwhile, make the chocolate mendiants. Draw around your 6 serving glasses (you don't want anything bigger than 6cm in diameter) on baking paper as a guideline. Place the paper on a tray that will fit in your fridge.

Put the chocolate and salt into a heatproof bowl and melt over a pan of just-simmering water (don't let the bowl touch the water) or in a microwave on a low heat. Remove from the heat and set the chocolate aside for 15 minutes to thicken slightly. Spoon the chocolate on to the circles on the baking paper (make them slightly smaller than the circles) and sprinkle each with some pistachios, apricots and a piece of Turkish delight. Place in the fridge for at least 15 minutes to set.

To finish off the coffee mix, beat the chilled coffee cream to loosen it up. Whip the double cream to soft peaks and fold into the coffee cream. Spoon a heaped tablespoon into each glass, followed by a teaspoon of the syrup. Alternate layers until the cream is used up (roughly 3–4 layers per glass). Chill for around 2 hours, or until serving. Top each cream with a mendiant lid, then serve.

Tips

Chocolate will split when it is melted at too hot a temperature. Make sure the water doesn't boil when melting in a bain-marie. If using a microwave, be sure to check and stir every few seconds.

The chocolate mix makes more than is required for the recipe, but these mendiants make wonderful edible gifts. They can be decorated with all sorts of dried fruit, nuts, chunks of soft toffee and seeds.

If your mendiants are too big to fit into the glass, use a small cookie cutter to trim. Dip the cookie cutter in hot water first, dry and use to cut the edge. Don't press down too hard or the mendiant will crack. The heat of the cookie cutter will cut the chocolate.

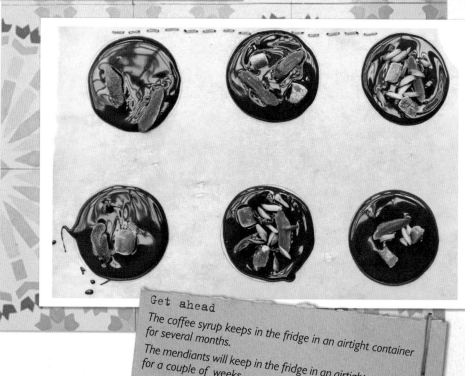

Get ahead

The coffee syrup keeps in the fridge in an airtight container for several months.

The mendiants will keep in the fridge in an airtight container for a couple of weeks.

Chocolate and courgette fondant fancies

Makes	Preparation time:	Resting time:	Baking time:
25 fondants	30 minutes	1 hour	60–80 minutes

Don't be put off by the idea of courgette in your cake. Like carrot, it makes for an extra-moist cake. The combination of hazelnut and chocolate reminds me of the famous shop-bought spread; you could look at these fondants as a more wholesome and simplified variation.

4 eggs

250g caster sugar

150g plain flour

300g blanched ground hazelnuts

4 tsp baking powder

a pinch of sea salt

600g courgettes, trimmed and very finely grated

400g dark chocolate (70%), broken into pieces

5 tbsp vegetable or sunflower oil

70g icing sugar

100g white chocolate, broken into pieces

Equipment

a 23cm square tin, buttered and floured

Preheat the oven to 160°C (fan).

Put the eggs and caster sugar into a large bowl and whisk until thick and fluffy with an electric hand whisk, or use a standing mixer. In another bowl, mix together the flour, ground hazelnuts, baking powder and salt. Add the flour mixture to the eggs and sugar, and fold together quickly and lightly, then add the courgettes. Once they're incorporated evenly, pour the batter into the baking tin.

Bake in the centre of the oven for 60–80 minutes, or until a skewer comes out clean. Leave to cool for 5 minutes, then remove from the tin and transfer to a wire rack to cool completely. Refrigerate when it comes to room temperate, so it is firm upon cutting; this will help you get really straight edges on the cake.

Cut the cake into 4cm squares. Set the squares on a wire rack with baking paper underneath.

Meanwhile, melt the dark chocolate with 4 tablespoons of oil in a heatproof bowl set over a pan of just-simmering water (don't let the bowl touch the water). When melted, remove from the heat and stir in the icing sugar. The icing should be runny enough to drip down the cake.

Place a piece of cake on a slotted spoon, fork or angled spatula. Spoon over the chocolate icing evenly and leave to set on the wire rack for 30 minutes. If you find it easier, delicately ladle the chocolate icing over the top of the squares while they're on the rack, letting the excess drip on to the baking paper beneath (scooping up the icing to recycle for the other cakes).

Melt the white chocolate with 1 tablespoon of oil in a small heatproof bowl over a small pan of just-simmering water. Once the dark chocolate layer has set, drizzle the white chocolate decoration over the top and leave to set a further 10 minutes.

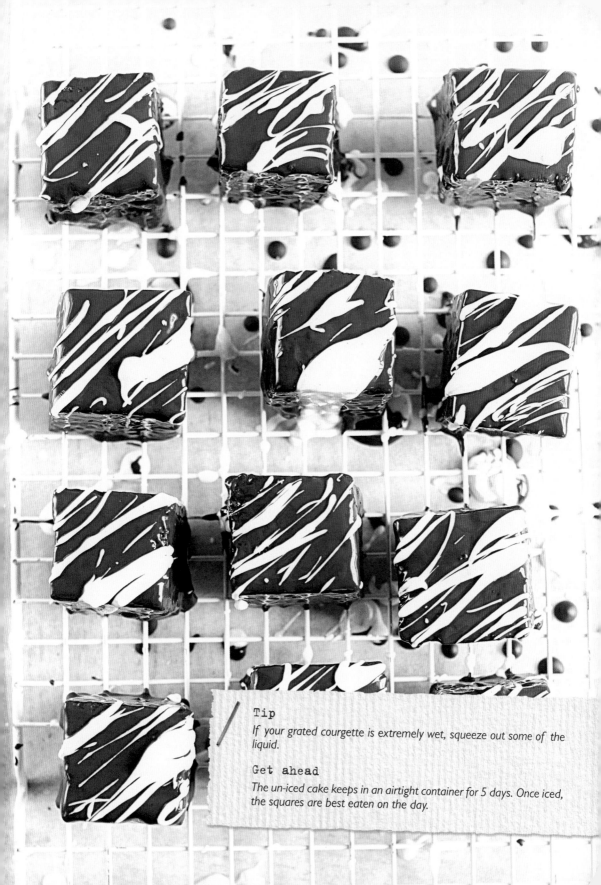

Tip

If your grated courgette is extremely wet, squeeze out some of the liquid.

Get ahead

The un-iced cake keeps in an airtight container for 5 days. Once iced, the squares are best eaten on the day.

Soft–serve ice cream with hazelnut caramel cone

Serves	Preparation time:	Cooking time:	Freezing time:
8	30 minutes	5 minutes	30–45 minutes

I love hearing the sound of the ice cream van. It reminds me of my childhood summers, when I would hound my mum to give me a pound so I could buy a 99 Flake. I still love eating a 99 Flake (although I must admit the chocolate always tastes a little dusty). The ice cream, however, is light, super-smooth and just dissolves in your mouth. You don't need a Mr Whippy machine in your kitchen to recreate the same experience; however, a sugar thermometer, an electric whisk (a standing mixer is the best) and a piping bag with a nozzle are essential.

250ml whipping cream

1 vanilla pod

25ml water

90g caster sugar

3 egg whites

8 ice cream waffle cones

For the caramel sauce

150g granulated sugar

150ml double cream

½ tsp sea salt

40g chopped and toasted hazelnuts (almonds, pecans or walnuts work too), plus 2 tbsp to serve

Equipment

a digital or sugar thermometer

a piping bag fitted with a wide star nozzle

8 tall glasses

Get ahead

The caramel will keep for a couple of months in the fridge in a sterilized jar.

To make the caramel, sprinkle a thin layer of granulated sugar over the bottom of a medium heavy-based pan and place on a medium heat. Once the sugar starts to melt, add some more sugar. Repeat until all the sugar has melted, swirling the caramel around in the pan (do not stir). When it's almost a Coca-Cola colour, turn the heat right down and add the double cream and salt (be careful as the caramel may splutter). Cook for 1–2 minutes until the temperature reaches 108°C – watch it constantly. Take the caramel off the heat and leave to cool for a couple of minutes, then mix in the chopped hazelnuts.

Put the whipping cream into a medium bowl. Halve the vanilla pod and scrape out the seeds, then add them to the cream and whip until it forms soft peaks. Cover with cling film and place in the fridge.

Pour the water and caster sugar into a small saucepan on a high heat. Bring to the boil, swirling to melt the sugar. Meanwhile, put the egg whites into a large bowl and whisk with an electric hand whisk or use a standing mixer. Measure the temperature of the sugar syrup with a digital thermometer once it starts to boil, and when the sugar syrup hits 126°C, slowly pour it on to the egg whites while whisking at a high speed. Continue to whisk for about 5 minutes, or until you have a firm, thick meringue and the bowl is cool.

Fold the chilled whipped cream into the meringue. Spoon into a large piping bag fitted with a wide star nozzle. Make room in your freezer for 8 tall glasses.

Place the waffle cones in the glasses and add a generous tablespoon of the caramel to each cone. Swirl each cone so that it coats the inside, then pipe the ice cream into the cone in a spiral motion. Place back in the freezer for 30–45 minutes, and serve with a sprinkling of chopped hazelnuts.

Shake—and—make ice cream and toppings

Makes	Preparation time:	Freezing time:
1 litre	15 minutes	approx. 1 hour

You might think making ice cream at home requires an ice cream machine or other gadgetry, but all you need are some bin bags, salt and ice: super high tech! This is the way it was done in the past. I used an old ice cream bucket when I worked in a restaurant in Sweden. It was a wooden bucket which you filled with ice and salt, and it had a second container to put the ice cream mix in. You then cranked a handle to turn the ice cream ingredients around.

The salt brings the temperature of the ice down. Shaking the ice cream also helps the mix to cool down, and makes it creamy. It's definitely a workout, but a fun thing to do with friends, when you can pass the effort around. Who would think that throwing some ingredients into a bin bag would make such a delicious result? Perhaps you'll have to try this for yourself to believe me!

500ml double cream

500ml whole milk

160g icing sugar

1 vanilla pod, halved lengthways and seeds scraped out

4 trays of ice cubes or 800g ready-made ice cubes

160g coarse sea salt

Equipment

a large reclosable food bag

2 heavy-duty bin liners

washing-up gloves

Place the double cream, milk, icing sugar and the seeds from the vanilla pod in your reclosable food bag. Make sure it's well sealed before massaging it to combine the ingredients.

Double-bag the bin liners and place the ice and the coarse salt inside. Shake a little before putting the ice cream bag inside. Put your washing-up gloves on. Shake the ice bag hard for at least 10 minutes, or until the mix has set soft.

You can eat the ice cream immediately by squeezing it out of the bag into a container, but for a firmer consistency place in the freezer for 1 hour.

Tips
You can change the ratio of milk to cream for more or less creaminess. Add candied fruits, nuts or chocolate chips for different flavourings.

Get ahead
Make the ice cream a few days ahead and store in the freezer until serving.

Ice cream toppings

Chocolate and hazelnut sauce

100g dark chocolate (70%)

75g shelled hazelnuts or nut butter (if using nut butter, don't add the butter below)

30g unsalted butter

2 tbsp honey

a pinch of sea salt

200ml double cream

Melt the chocolate in a heatproof bowl above a pan of just-simmering water (don't let the bowl touch the water). Grind the hazelnuts in a food processor to the finest powder you can achieve.

Add the butter to the chocolate, along with the honey and salt. Heat the double cream in a separate pan and pour over the chocolate. Stir together, add the hazelnut powder, mix well and serve.

Cherry compote

1 x 440g tin of stoneless black cherries in syrup

1 vanilla pod

½ tsp almond essence

Heat the cherries in their syrup in a pan. Split the vanilla pod, scrape out the seeds and add them to the pan, along with the pod, then simmer for 10 minutes. Stir in the almond essence, remove the pod and serve.

Caramel popcorn

½ tbsp salted butter

40g popcorn kernels

For the salted butter caramel

75g granulated sugar

50ml double cream

1 heaped tbsp golden syrup

a knob of unsalted butter

½ tsp sea salt

Melt the salted butter in a large pan with a lid over a medium heat. Turn the heat up to medium-high, add the popcorn kernels and place the lid on the pan. When you hear the popcorn popping, you are in action.

Shake the pan to make sure all the kernels have popped. Once they sound like they have stopped popping, remove from the heat and set aside in a bowl.

Add half the sugar to a medium saucepan with 2 tablespoons of water. Place on a high heat and leave to melt. Do not stir, but swirl the pan around if needed. Once the caramel becomes a dark reddish brown, take the pan off the heat and add the rest of the sugar, the double cream, golden syrup, unsalted butter and salt.

Put the saucepan back on the heat. Be careful not to stand over it as the caramel will steam and bubble a lot. Swirl the pan around before turning the heat down to medium. Cook for 3–4 minutes, or until it reaches 120°C and is rich, thick and unctuous.

Stir the popcorn into the caramel, then spread the popcorn out on a lined baking tray to cool. Break it up to serve.

Tropical knickerbocker glory

Serves	Preparation time:	Freezing time:	Cooking time:
4	40 minutes	6 hours	15 minutes

This recipe is a twist on one of my favourite Malaysian desserts, *cendol*. *Cendol* is a bright green sweet noodle, usually made with mung-bean flour and pandan leaf. The flavour and colour comes from the pandan leaf, which has an aromatic sweet almond and vanilla perfume. The noodles are then mixed with shaved ice and red beans and doused with coconut milk.

I've switched some of the ingredients (pandan leaf and mung-bean flour) for ones that are easy to buy in the supermarket (rice flour, cornflour and tropical juice). There are no red beans in sight, but instead a colourful assortment of tropical fruits. No need for an ice machine to shave ice either; a quick-to-make coconut granita replaces that.

6 ripe passion fruits

½ a small mango

½ a galia or cantaloupe melon

juice and zest of 1 lime

For the coconut granita

100g caster sugar

100ml water

1 x 400ml tin of coconut milk

For the tropical *cendol*

25g rice flour

25g cornflour

250ml tropical or exotic fruit juice

Equipment

a medium-sized piping or
food bag

4 sundae glasses

Tip

The granita can be made up to 2–3 weeks in advance. Just remove from the freezer for about 15 minutes to soften if frozen solid.

To make the coconut granita, dissolve the sugar in the water in a medium saucepan over a low heat, swirling the pan gently, then bring to a simmer for 1 minute. Take off the heat and stir in the coconut milk. Pour the mix into a plastic lidded container. Place in the freezer and leave for 6 hours, forking every hour or so after the first 2 hours (make sure you fork the sides too, otherwise it will freeze solid). Once the mixture is firm, cover or wrap tightly in cling film.

To make the tropical *cendol*, place the flours in a small saucepan. Whisk the fruit juice into the flours, then cook over a medium heat for 8–10 minutes, or until the mixture becomes very thick and glossy, whisking continuously. Take off the heat and leave for 2 minutes.

Prepare a large bowl full of iced water. Transfer the *cendol* to a medium-sized piping or food bag and snip off a small corner. Wearing washing-up gloves (as the mixture in the bag is still very hot), pipe the cendol in long pieces straight into the iced water. Set aside for 15 minutes.

Meanwhile, prepare the fruit. Remove the pulp from the passion fruits and put into a large bowl. Stone the mango and deseed the melon, then chop the flesh into bite-size pieces. Toss the fruit with the lime juice and zest (saving a little zest for the garnish).

When ready to serve, take 4 sundae glasses, fork up the granita and place some at the bottom of each glass. Drain the water from the *cendol* and add some to each glass, then add a spoonful of fruit. Add another layer of granita, *cendol* and fruit, then sprinkle with a little lime zest. Serve immediately.

Mini ice pops

Makes	Preparation time:	Cooking time:	Freezing time:
16	5 minutes	10 minutes	2 hours

A DIY attitude is required for this recipe. I wanted to come up with an ice pop mould that everyone could make out of things they would have at home: an ice cube tray and cardboard (a cereal box works well). These little fruit pops are a refreshing way to finish a meal (similar to the ones that posh restaurants serve before dessert, to refresh the palate) or to have on a hot summer's day.

400g frozen mixed summer berries

75g icing sugar

1 tbsp roasted chopped hazelnuts

1 tbsp caraway seeds, toasted

1 tbsp hundreds and thousands

1 tbsp chocolate sprinkles

Equipment

1 piece of cardboard

a 16-hole ice cube tray

4 bulldog clips

16 lollipop sticks

Cut a piece of cardboard to the size of the top of your ice cube tray. Wrap the cardboard thoroughly in cling film, place over the ice cube tray and use a stencil knife or a pair of scissors to make 16 little slits in the cardboard over the centre of the cubes on the tray.

Put the berries and icing sugar into a medium saucepan on a medium heat, cover with a lid and cook for about 10 minutes. Transfer to a blender and whizz till smooth, then pour through a sieve into a jug. Pour the coulis into the ice cube tray. Place the cardboard lid on the ice cube tray, secure with the bulldog clips, then place the lollipop sticks in the slits. Place in the freezer for 2 hours, or until frozen solid.

Remove from the freezer 10 minutes before serving and place in the fridge. Put the nuts, seeds and sprinkles into separate bowls, and when ready to serve carefully remove the cardboard and dunk the fruit pops in your topping of choice.

Tip

Lightly oil the cling film used to wrap around the cardboard – this will help stop the frozen coulis sticking.

Get ahead

The fruit pops can be made 2–3 weeks in advance.

miso toffee
cherry tomatoes

Potato...

BORJA

BY AIR MAIL
PAR AVION

Homemade Treats

Pine nut marzipan
truffles

Last, but certainly not least, I leave you with my final chapter. From cookies (page 240) and Swedish-style buns (page 224), to truffles (pages 216 and 218) and sweet chilli sauce (page 251): even the most unstoppable of cooks (myself included) have been tempted to buy some of these rather than make them at home. But homemade is always so much better then shop-bought, and while they might be more time-consuming to make, you'll definitely reap the rewards later.

From my time in France and beyond, the aperitif culture will always stick with me, and in this chapter you'll discover some impressive recipes for serving in that oft-neglected time before a meal. There's my home-cured duck breast (page 220), from which you can simply slice off some slivers for an impromptu aperitif. Or my homemade grissini (page 232), so unbelievably simple, you'll wonder why you never bothered making your own before.

Edible gifts come in many guises, and my chocolate bark (page 212) makes for a really speedy lunchbox treat for kids or even ever-so-lucky other halves. Then there are the cook's cheats to make everyday life a little bit more gourmet; take my stock cubes (page 248), or my homemade cottage cheese (page 246) and put your own stamp on them when you use them.

This chapter is filled with a selection of my recipes I have collected along the way, many of which have become my most trusted and used. I hope they become yours too.

Chocolate bark

Preparation time:
5 minutes

Cooking time:
5 minutes

Cooling time:
1 hour

Making your own chocolate bark couldn't be simpler. Great for a snack, after-dinner chocolates or the perfect edible gift.

200g dark chocolate (70%), broken into pieces

15g mixed seeds (e.g. sunflower, pumpkin and sesame)

15g pistachio kernels

20g dried cranberries

Put the chocolate into a heatproof bowl and place over a pan of just-simmering water (don't let the bowl touch the water). Stir occasionally until melted. Line a tray with baking paper and pour the chocolate on to it, then spread with a spatula or palette knife into a rectangle about 18cm x 22cm and around 0.5cm thick.

Immediately sprinkle the seeds, pistachios and cranberries evenly over the top. Transfer to the fridge to set for at least 1 hour. Once set, break the bark up into jagged pieces.

Tip
The toppings you can use for this are endless. I usually see what I have left over in my cupboard – from dried apricots, figs or freeze-dried fruit (great for colour), to hazelnuts, pecans and sugar sprinkles.

Get ahead
Chocolate bark keeps in the fridge for up to 2 weeks.

Gorgonzola and ricotta sfogliatella

Makes
12

Preparation time:
20 minutes

Baking time:
20–25 minutes

Making *sfogliatella* the traditional way is nearly as difficult as pronouncing the word. The traditional method calls for making a pastry and rolling it incredibly thinly. Then it is rolled up, chilled, formed into cone shapes and filled with a semolina and ricotta cream that is studded with candied fruits ... basically, unless you have a large extended Italian family to help you with this, you'll be in the kitchen all day.

Not wanting to be defeated by a complicated technique, I set about finding a simple version which would still have the classic crispy layered pastry. Combining thinly rolled-out puff pastry and filo pastry seems to do the trick. I like to fill these with apple and a rich ricotta and Gorgonzola cream, which makes them perfect to kick off an evening of entertaining.

a little flour for dusting

215g ready-rolled puff pastry

2 sheets of filo pastry
(sheet size 30cm x 40cm)

1 egg, beaten, for egg wash

1 small apple

75g ricotta cheese

50g Gorgonzola cheese

Dust the work surface with flour. Take the rectangle of puff pastry and place it in a portrait position. Dust the top of the pastry with a little flour and roll out to the size of the sheet of filo pastry. The pastry should end up a couple of millimetres thick. Sweep off the excess flour before brushing with egg wash. Place a sheet of filo over the top. Turn over and repeat with the other sheet of filo on the other side. Cut the pastry into 2.5cm strips using a pizza cutter.

Preheat the oven to 180°C (fan).

Quarter the apple, then cut each quarter into two slices. Cut each slice in half, so you're left with pieces with a wider and slimmer end. Mix the ricotta and Gorgonzola together in a small bowl.

Brush egg wash all over the surface of a strip of pastry. Place a piece of apple at the end. Roll the strip up around the apple, making each fold slightly askew from the previous one. You will end up with a cone of pastry, with the apple at one end and a space at the other.

Push a teaspoon of the cheese mixture into the space, then seal both ends to encase the apple and cheese, using some egg wash to stick the pastry in place. Place on a baking tray lined with baking paper and repeat with the remaining ingredients.

Brush the outside of the pastries with egg wash before placing in the oven. Bake for 20–25 minutes, or until golden and crisp.

Tip
If the puff pastry is very soft, put a sheet of baking paper on top, roll it up and place in the fridge for 10 minutes.

Raw fig truffles

Makes	Preparation time:	Cooking time:	Chilling time:
12	20 minutes	5 minutes	1 hour

I love fresh figs: they're like sweets for me. When I lived in Paris I would go to my local market and pick up a bag, and by the time I got home they would be gone. It's difficult to find perfectly ripe figs when they're not in season, so for the rest of the year I have to get my fig fix with the dried version. Dried figs are more intense and sweeter than the fresh ones, and pair beautifully with bitter dark chocolate.

85g dried figs

85g Medjool dates, stones removed

40g pistachio kernels

20g soft unsalted butter

½ tsp sea salt

100g dark chocolate (70%)

70g blanched almonds, toasted and finely chopped

Remove and discard the tough stalks from the tops of the figs. Chop the figs, then place in a food processor with the dates, pistachio kernels, butter and salt. Whizz until they form a paste. Tip the paste out of the processor and roll into 12 small truffle-sized balls, then place on a tray.

Put the chocolate into a heatproof bowl over a pan of just-simmering water (don't let the bowl touch the water). Leave to melt. Place the chopped almonds on a plate.

Dip the truffle balls into the melted chocolate one at a time, using a couple of forks to coat well. Immediately transfer to the chopped almonds and roll to coat. Place on a plate or a small baking tray lined with cling film, then coat the remaining truffles. Put into the fridge to set for 1 hour.

Tip
Experiment with other dried fruit or nuts to fill or coat your truffles.

Get ahead
These keep well in the fridge for a week or so in an airtight container. You can also freeze them before coating them with chocolate. They are good uncoated too.

Pine nut marzipan truffles

Makes 20–24	Preparation time: 20 minutes	Cooking time: 10 minutes

When you're planning the perfect meal, it's good to think about balance. Sometimes a traditional dessert, like a slice of cake or pudding, is just too heavy. Some homemade chocolate truffles and a small digestif, however, will stop your guests feeling like they need to be forklifted home. Try my little pine nut marzipan truffles for a lighter finale, or make a double batch and offer them as excellent edible gifts.

250g pine nuts, toasted

85g caster sugar

85g icing sugar

1 egg

55g ground almonds

a generous pinch of sea salt

200g dark chocolate (70%), chopped

Grind 180g of pine nuts in a blender until fine (but don't go so far that you end up with pine nut butter!).

Put a large heatproof bowl over a pan of just-simmering water (don't let the bowl touch the water). Place the sugars in the bowl, then whisk in the egg and continue whisking until the mixture turns pale and creamy. Take off the heat and let it cool a little.

Stir in the ground pine nuts, along with the almonds and salt, and continue stirring until you have a smooth dough and the mixture is thoroughly cool. Form the dough into little balls in the palm of your hand, about the size of truffles.

Bring the pan of water up to a simmer again. Place the chocolate in a clean heatproof bowl and melt it over the water.

Line a baking tray with some cling film. Dip the marzipan balls in the chocolate using a truffle fork, or simply dunk them in the chocolate and fish them out with a fork or palette knife. Place on the tray and scatter with the remaining pine nuts. Leave to dry, then place in the fridge to set.

Tip
If you find the flavour of the pine nuts too intense, you can use 120g pine nuts and 120g almonds in the marzipan balls.

Get ahead
These keep well in the fridge for a week or so in a an airtight container. You can also freeze them.

Spiced duck ham

Makes	Preparation time:	Curing time:
1 duck breast	15 minutes	17 days

Making your own charcuterie couldn't be easier. The only thing you have to exercise is a little patience. As the saying goes, 'All good things come to those who wait' (the duck has to hang for a little over two weeks before it's ready). But, at the end of this recipe, you'll be left with your own delicious cured duck breast.

300g coarse sea salt

200g granulated sugar

1 duck breast (approx. 500g)

2 tbsp freshly ground pepper (I use a mixture of black, Szechuan and white pepper)

1 juniper berry, crushed

zest of 1 orange

Equipment
a muslin cloth

Mix the salt and sugar together. Cut a large piece of cling film, and place half the salt-sugar mix in the middle. Place the duck breast on top. Cover with the rest of the salt-sugar mix and wrap up tightly. Leave in the fridge for 72 hours.

Rinse the duck with cold water and pat dry with some kitchen towel. Rub the spices and orange zest into the duck breast, then wrap it loosely in a muslin cloth or a clean tea towel and hang it in the fridge. Leave for 14 days.

Unwrap and serve in very thin slices with a fresh green salad or just on its own with some crusty bread and cornichons.

Tip
Make sure the meat is completely covered by the salt and sugar mix, so that it dries out evenly.

Get ahead
The duck will continue to cure and dry in the fridge for 6 – 8 weeks.

Soft steamed buns

Makes 8 dumplings
(serves 4 as
a main course)

Preparation time:
40 minutes

Resting time:
1 hour 15 minutes

Cooking time:
30–40 minutes

Eating *cha sui bao*, the steamed Chinese buns filled with roast pork, was part of my childhood. The fluffy light dough encasing savoury, sticky and slightly sweet roast meat was one of my brother's and my favourites, growing up. The dumpling dough makes the perfect vehicle for using up leftovers. Serve some steamed tenderstem broccoli on the side, and the buns are no longer simply a snack but a delicious meal in themselves.

2 tbsp vegetable oil, for frying

500ml good-quality beef stock (or other stock, depending on meat used)

sweet chilli sauce (see page 251), to serve

For the bun dough

160g plain flour, plus extra for dusting

1 tbsp milk powder

1½ tbsp caster sugar

1 scant tsp fast-action yeast

1 tsp baking powder

a pinch of sea salt

90ml warm water

1 tbsp vegetable oil

For the filling

140g leftover roast meat, such as pork

1 spring onion

½ a carrot

1 tbsp tomato purée

1 tbsp light soy sauce

½ tsp freshly ground pepper

Put the dry ingredients for the bun dough into a large bowl. Mix together, then make a well in the centre and add the warm water. Use a spoon to bring together, then turn out and knead for 2–3 minutes, or until you have a smooth dough. Place in a bowl greased with vegetable oil and cover with a tea towel or cling film. Leave to rise for 45 minutes, or until nearly doubled in size.

Make the filling by trimming the fat from the leftover roast meat, then cutting the meat into 2mm cubes. Thinly slice the spring onion and cut the carrot into 2mm cubes. Put them all into a small bowl, add the tomato purée, soy sauce and pepper, and mix well.

Dust the work surface and your hands with flour. Divide the dough into two. Roll the first piece into a fat sausage and cut it into 4 equal parts. Roll each part into a ball, then flatten into a circle. Put a heaped tablespoon of filling into the middle of each one. Stretch the dough over the filling and squeeze the top together so that they're sealed. Dip the tops of the dumplings in flour (to stop them sticking) and place seam side down on a tray. Repeat with the rest of the dough, and leave to rise for 30 minutes.

Put the oil into a large non-stick pan with a vented lid on a medium heat. Place the dumplings seam side down in the pan and fry for a couple of minutes, or until the dumplings have developed a golden crust on the bottom. Add the stock, bring to the boil and cover with the lid. Cook for 30–40 minutes, or until you hear a sizzling noise. Once the pan begins to sizzle it means the stock has evaporated. Cook for another minute to crisp up the base of the dumplings, then serve immediately with a spoon of sweet chilli sauce.

Tip
For a vegetarian version, replace the meat with finely chopped button mushrooms.

Lemon, dill and fish roe bullar

Makes	Preparation time:	Proving time:	Cooking time:
22–24 buns	20 minutes	1½ hours	20 minutes

The Swedes love their buns. You can't go into a bakery, café or petrol station without finding a *kanelbulle* or *kardemummabulle* (cinnamon or cardamom bun). *Bulle*, quite simply, means bun or ball (Swedish meatballs are called *köttbullar*, for instance). These savoury versions make a great snack on the go, and use some of the perennial flavours found in Swedish cuisine: dill, lemon and fish roe.

270ml lukewarm whole milk

75g caster sugar

½ tsp sea salt

90g unsalted butter, melted

2 eggs, 1 beaten for egg wash

2 tsp fast-action yeast

500g strong white bread flour, plus extra to knead

400g cream cheese

4 tbsp finely chopped fresh dill

zest of 1 unwaxed lemon

6 tbsp lumpfish caviar

Mix the milk, sugar, salt, butter, 1 egg and yeast together in the bowl of a mixer fitted with a dough hook. When combined, add the flour in two batches. Knead for 10 minutes until it comes together, adding a little more flour if necessary.

When the dough is nice and stretchy, form it into a ball with your hands. Cover with a clean damp tea towel or cloth and set aside in a warmish place for about 1 hour, or until it doubles in size.

Dust the work surface lightly with flour. Divide the dough into 2 balls (I find this easier to roll out in 2 batches; alternatively, you can just save the other half for another day).

Roll the dough into a rectangle about 40cm x 35cm and around 0.5cm thick. Spread half the cream cheese in an even layer on top, then sprinkle on half the dill, half the lemon zest and dot over half the fish roe.

Fold into thirds, lengthwise, first lifting a third of the dough towards the middle, then folding the top third down so it aligns with the bottom edge of the dough. Cut the dough into strips about 3cm wide using a pizza cutter or knife, then cut each strip down the middle until 2cm from the top, as if you're making a pair of trousers. Twist each strip, then twist each pair of strips together and into a bun shape, tucking the ends underneath. Place on a lined baking tray.

Repeat with the remaining dough, then brush with egg wash and leave to prove for about 30 minutes. Brush with egg wash a second time before putting in the oven.

Preheat the oven to 200°C (fan) and bake for 15–20 minutes, until golden. Place on a wire rack and leave to cool. These are best eaten slightly warm and fresh on the day.

Tip

For the traditional kanelbullar *(cinnamon buns), replace the topping ingredients with 300g of soft butter, 160g of light brown sugar and 2 tablespoons of ground cinnamon. Beat the ingredients together before spreading on top of dough, then follow the same procedure.*

Savoury gems

Makes
50

Preparation time:
45 minutes

Cooking time:
10–12 minutes

Iced gems would always appear in a bowl on the party buffet table when I was a kid. Those little round biscuits topped with candy-coloured icing were very hard to resist. Sometimes memories are best left in the past, however, as when I tasted them recently I realized how easily satisfied I was with food as a child. I was no food connoisseur back then! Despite the fact shop-bought ones can be a little disappointing, homemade savoury ones are the perfect way to kick off a party. These bite-size buttery crackers topped with colourful (all natural!) toppings are a treat for both old and young.

For the cracker bases

80g plain flour

75g wholemeal plain flour

½ tsp sea salt

1 tbsp caster sugar

1 tsp paprika

80g cold butter, cubed

2 tsp vodka

For the devilled egg

3 large eggs

2 tbsp mayonnaise (see page 249)

1 tsp English mustard

sea salt and freshly ground pepper

For the avocado cream

1 ripe avocado

1 tsp lime juice or lemon juice

a pinch of salt

For the harissa cream cheese

1 tsp harissa paste

100g cream cheese or mascarpone cheese

Equipment

3cm cutter

3 piping bags with a 4–5mm star nozzle

Preheat the oven to 170°C (fan). To make the cracker bases, mix together the flours, salt, sugar and paprika in a large bowl, then rub the butter in with your fingers until you have a sandy texture. Add the vodka and bring the mix together into a ball. Roll out with a rolling pin to 5mm thickness between two sheets of baking paper.

Line a baking tray with baking paper. With the cutter, stamp out 50 cookies, re-rolling the dough as necessary. Put on the tray and bake for 10–12 minutes, or until the bases are golden. Take out of the oven and transfer to a wire rack to cool.

Meanwhile, make the savoury creams. For the devilled egg cream, place the eggs in a pan of boiling water and boil for 10 minutes. Remove with a slotted spoon and run under cold water to cool. Peel the eggs and remove the yolk from the white (discarding the white). Mix the yolks with the mayonnaise, mustard and salt and pepper to taste. Blend to a purée (a small food processor is ideal for this) and set aside.

Scoop the flesh out of the avocado into a small bowl, add the lime or lemon juice and salt, then mix and blend to a purée. In a separate bowl, mix the harissa into the cheese and blend this to a purée too.

Place the devilled egg purée into a piping bag with the star nozzle and pipe little blobs on to a third of the cooled crackers. Clean the nozzle, then repeat with the other purées and crackers.

Tips

If the pastry becomes too soft when handling, place in the freezer for 5 minutes and run your hands under cold water.

Adding vodka to the pastry will make for a flakier pastry than using ice-cold water. The alcohol evaporates when baked.

Mini focaccia buns

Makes	Preparation time:	Proving time:	Baking time:
10 buns	20 minutes	1 hour	20 minutes

The Italians, like the French, are strong supporters of tradition, particularly when it comes to gastronomy and timeless recipes. So apologies in advance for these delightful little focaccia buns, which I doubt you will have previously encountered in a trattoria. Being small, these buns take a lot less time to prove and cook, meaning there will be fresh bread on the table quicker than you can say *mamma mia*. They are also great for using up all those little bits lurking in the back of the fridge.

250g strong white bread flour, plus extra to dust

4g or 1 tsp fast-action yeast

sea salt

170ml lukewarm water

olive oil

various garnishes, such as cubed cheese (e.g. taleggio, goat's cheese, Gorgonzola), fresh rosemary, olives, thinly sliced garlic, marinated tomatoes or artichokes, jalapeño chillies, cubes of cooked potato or butternut squash

In a large bowl, mix together the dry ingredients and 1 teaspoon of sea salt. Make a well in the middle and pour in the warm water. Mix until you have a rough dough. Turn out and knead for about 10 minutes, or until soft and smooth.

Place in an oiled bowl and cover with a clean damp tea towel. Leave to rise in a warm place for 30 minutes, or until doubled in size.

Punch down the dough. Roll into a sausage on a lightly floured surface and cut into 10 pieces, then roll each piece into a ball. Poke your thumb in the middle to make a hole, fill with a teaspoon of olive oil and stick in the garnish. Make sure to press the garnish down very firmly (the buns will puff up and push out the topping otherwise). Place them on a lined baking tray.

Leave to rise for 30 minutes, or until doubled in size. Preheat the oven to 200°C (fan). Before placing in the oven, firmly push the garnish into the bun once more and drizzle with a little more olive oil. Sprinkle with sea salt.

Bake for 20 minutes, or until golden. Tap the base to check if they are cooked: they should sound hollow.

Get ahead
The dough can be left overnight in the fridge for the first prove.
The buns keep for up to 2 days; reheat in a low oven to freshen them up.
The buns also freeze well. Defrost and reheat in a low oven.

Grissini

Makes:	Preparation time:	Resting time:	Baking time:
16–25	15 minutes	1–2 hours	12–15 minutes

Italy's cuisine, like that of France, is considered one of the world's greatest, and although I haven't spent nearly as much time in Italy as I have done in France, I'm very fond of the food. I do have one pet hate, however, which I discovered while eating out on many of my trips there: those mass-produced, plastic-packaged grissini sticks that are served in bread baskets at restaurants. These grissini are dry, flavourless and, for me, like eating compressed sawdust. Anyway, enough ranting! I decided to put together a mini guide on how to make the most fantastic array of grissini, fit for a king or queen's bread basket.

For the basic dough

250g strong white bread flour, plus extra for dusting

½ tsp fast-action yeast

¾ tsp sea salt

½ tsp caster sugar

165ml warm water

Equipment

a lightly oiled bowl

a pizza cutter

Mix the dry ingredients in a large bowl, make a well in the centre and pour in the warm water. Stir the ingredients together, then use your hand to knead the mixture for about 5 minutes. The dough will be quite wet, but don't be tempted to add flour: the more you knead it, the less wet it will become. When the dough comes together into a small ball (but is still sticky), place it in a lightly oiled bowl. Cover with cling film and leave in a warm place for 1 hour, until it doubles in size.

Preheat the oven to 200°C (fan). Dust the work surface with some flour and roll out the dough to a 30cm x 25cm rectangle, about 1cm thick. Cut with a pizza cutter into 1cm-wide strips. Place the sticks on a baking tray lined with baking paper, leaving 2cm between them.

Bake in the oven on the middle shelf for 12–15 minutes, or until golden and crisp. Remove to a wire rack and leave to cool slightly before eating. Wait until completely cool before storing in an airtight container.

Apple and fig

½ an apple, cut into 2mm cubes

3 dried figs, hard knobbly bit removed and thinly sliced

1 x basic dough (above)

Add the apple cubes and dried figs to the dough after mixing in the water and before kneading. Repeat the same process as above.

Rye, caraway and Cheddar

75g rye flour

175g strong white bread flour plus extra for dusting

½ tsp fast-action yeast

¾ tsp sea salt

½ tsp caster sugar

165ml warm water

75g mature Cheddar, cut into small cubes

1 tsp caraway seeds, plus ½ tsp to garnish

Mix the two flours, yeast, salt and sugar in a large bowl, then add the water, stir and knead as in the basic grissini recipe. Add the Cheddar cubes and caraway seeds towards the end of the kneading time so that they are evenly incorporated. Let the dough rest as before, then roll it out to a 25cm square and cut into 16 strips roughly 1.5cm wide. Scatter with a few of the remaining caraway seeds, pressing them in lightly. Spread out on a baking tray, and bake and cool as before.

Raspberry and dark chocolate 'pocky'

100g fresh raspberries

65–90ml warm water

250g strong white bread flour, plus extra for dusting

½ tsp fast-action yeast

½ tsp sea salt

1 tbsp caster sugar

200g dark chocolate (70%)

Place the raspberries in the warm water and crush lightly with a fork. Mix the flour, yeast, salt and sugar in a large bowl, then add the raspberries and their liquid. Stir, then knead, let the dough rest, roll out and bake as in the basic grissini recipe.

Once baked, leave to cool slightly while you melt the chocolate. Cut the chocolate into small pieces and place in a heatproof bowl above a pan of just-simmering water (don't let the bowl touch the water). Use a spoon to pour the melted chocolate over half of each of the breadsticks. Leave to set in the fridge for 15 minutes on a baking tray lined with baking paper.

Pistachio, sesame, white chocolate and wasabi

250g strong white bread flour, plus extra for dusting

20g ground pistachio kernels

½ tsp fast-action yeast

¾ tsp sea salt

½ tsp caster sugar

165ml warm water

1 tbsp black sesame seeds

100g white chocolate

2 tsp wasabi powder

Mix the flour, ground pistachios, yeast, salt and sugar in a large bowl. Add the water, then stir, knead and let the dough rest as in the basic grissini recipe. Roll the dough out into a 25cm square and cut into 16 strips roughly 1.5cm wide. Scatter with the sesame seeds. Spread out on a baking tray, and bake and cool as before.

Once baked, leave to cool slightly while you melt the white chocolate. Cut the chocolate into small pieces and place in a heatproof bowl above a pan of just-simmering water (don't let the bowl touch the water). Add the wasabi to the melted chocolate and stir, then use a spoon to drizzle it haphazardly over the top of the sticks. Leave to set in the fridge for 15 minutes on a baking tray lined with baking paper.

Raspberry and dark chocolate 'pocky'

Apple and fig

Grissini

Pistachio, sesame, white chocolate and wasabi

Pizza grissini

1 tsp tomato purée

150ml warm water

250g white strong bread flour, plus extra for dusting

½ tsp fast-action yeast

¾ tsp sea salt

½ tsp caster sugar

50g sundried tomatoes, finely chopped

1 tbsp dried oregano

Mix the tomato purée with the water in a small bowl. Mix the flour, yeast, salt and sugar in a separate large bowl. Add the sundried tomatoes, oregano and tomato purée liquid, then stir, knead, let the dough rest, roll out and bake the dough as on page 232.

No-knead herby gluten-free grissini

400g gluten-free plain white flour blend (I use Doves Farm)

1 tsp fast-action yeast

1½ tsp sea salt

2 tsp caster sugar

2 tsp nigella seeds

2 tsp dried mint

2 tsp dried thyme

300ml warm water

1 egg, beaten, for egg wash

Mix the dry ingredients together in a large bowl and add the water, mixing together until well incorporated. Roll into a ball and leave to rest for 2 hours in a lightly oiled bowl covered with cling film.

Preheat the oven to 200°C (fan). Remove the dough from the bowl and divide into 20 pieces. Roll each piece into a ball, then into the shape of a breadstick on your board. Place on a baking tray lined with baking paper and brush with the egg wash, then bake as on page 232.

Tips

Grissini are great as both a sweet and a savoury finger food. Here are some ideas to pimp up your basic recipe breadsticks for a party:

- *Stick the following on the end of them: raspberries; hard-boiled quail eggs dipped in sesame seeds; little mozzarella cheese bocconcini*
- *Wrap them in melon ribbons and Parma ham*
- *Spread cream cheese along one end, then wrap peeled apple ribbons around the tip*

Get ahead

If you don't manage to nibble through the whole batch in one go, like I do, then these will keep in an airtight container for a couple of days.

Rye and treacle quick bread with whipped homemade butter

Makes 1 loaf (using a 1lb loaf tin)	Preparation time 15 minutes	Cooking time 30 minutes

This is the perfect loaf for those with limited patience who love fresh bread. Unlike a traditional loaf this bread relies on bicarbonate of soda rather than yeast, and as little mixing as possible to make a soft and tender crumb. With a slightly sweet and bitter note from the treacle, it goes down a treat when warm and buttered. Homemade butter might seem like taking it too far but there's nothing to it apart from over-whipping the cream (plus the excess buttermilk comes in handy for the bread).

For the whipped butter
500ml double cream
2 pinches of sea salt
3 tbsp finely chopped chives

For the quick bread
125g plain flour
125g rye or wholemeal flour
1 tsp bicarbonate of soda
1 tbsp brown sugar
1 tsp ground sea salt flakes
40–70ml plain yoghurt
75g treacle
1 tbsp rolled oats

Equipment
a 450g loaf tin, greased and floured

Preheat the oven to 180°C (fan).

Whisk the double cream on a high speed in a freestanding mixer with whisk attachment, until it separates to butter solids and buttermilk – this takes about 5 minutes. Drain off the buttermilk and set aside. Continue to whip the remaining butter until soft and fluffy, adding the salt and chopped chives.

Mix together the flours, bicarbonate of soda, brown sugar and salt flakes in a large bowl. Make a well in the centre. Measure out the buttermilk and add enough yoghurt to bring the weight up to 200g. Pour the buttermilk and yoghurt into the centre of the dry ingredients, mix together and add the treacle. Mix together until everything is incorporated. Try not to overwork it. Put the mixture into the tin and spread it out so that it is level. Sprinkle with oats.

Bake for 30 minutes, or until the skewer comes out clean from the centre. Leave to cool for 5 minutes before taking out of the tin. Cover with a damp tea towel while cooling. Serve with the butter on the side.

Tips
Best eaten while warm or the following day toasted.

If you want to avoid making the butter, replace the buttermilk and yoghurt in the bread recipe with a combination of 100ml whole milk and 100g plain yoghurt.

Dark chocolate and cherry cookies

Makes	Preparation time:	Freezing time:	Baking time:
16	10 minutes	30–45 minutes	12–14 minutes

I woke up one morning with an overwhelming craving for a deep dark chocolate cookie studded with cherries. Most importantly, it had to have the right texture: crisp on the edges and chewy in the middle. A few factors are involved in making the perfect chewy cookie: baking for the right amount of time at the right temperature; and using dark brown sugar, which makes for a moister cookie.

100g salted butter

80g dark brown soft sugar

80g light brown soft sugar

½ tsp sea salt

100g plain flour

2½ tbsp cocoa powder (20g)

½ tsp baking powder

1 egg

½ tsp bitter almond essence

100g dark chocolate (70%), roughly chopped into small pieces

100g tinned black stoneless cherries (drained weight), chopped in half

Melt the butter, sugars and salt in a medium saucepan, then leave to cool slightly.

Sift the plain flour, cocoa powder and baking powder into a bowl and mix together. Make a well in the centre, add the egg and almond essence and begin to mix. Pour in the slightly cooled butter and sugar. Mix together until there are no lumps.

Lay out a large piece of cling film on a small baking tray on your work surface. Pour the cookie mix on to the film and spread into a neat square, about 2cm thick. Use the excess cling film to cover the batter and place in the freezer on the tray for 30–45 minutes (or in the fridge for 1–2 hours), until firm enough to cut into 16 squares.

Preheat the oven to 170°C (fan). Line two large baking trays with baking paper and place the cookie squares on them, leaving a 3–4 cm gap between each cookie (they will spread out a fair bit as they cook). Press the chocolate and cherries lightly into the cookies. Bake for 12–14 minutes, or until slightly crisp on the outside but still soft in the middle (they will harden when they cool). Leave on the baking tray for 10 minutes when you remove them from the oven, then use a fish slice or spatula to transfer to a wire rack to cool.

Tip

For a plain cookie, replace the cocoa powder with plain flour. The cherries and chocolate can be replaced with other flavourings, such as white chocolate and dried cranberries, or dark chocolate and walnuts.

Get ahead

The cookies freeze well, either cooked or as a dough. Add an extra 5 minutes to the cooking time if baking from frozen.

These are best eaten on the day you bake them.

THESE WILD GARLIC FLOWERS
WOULD BE DELICIOUS
IN AN OMELETTE

STRAWBERRIES -
PERFECT FOR CAKE RECIPE

LOVE THE NAME OF
THESE CUCUMBERS

MY KIND OF HEAVEN -
CHEESE!

NOTHING BEATS GETTING A
BEAUTIFUL BUNCH OF FLOWERS

OYSTERS WITH A
BLOODY MARY DRESSING

HUGE SEAFOOD PLATTER

A SMALL HANDFUL
OF LINGONBERRIES -
ENOUGH FOR ME ☺

AMAZING WHAT YOU CAN
GROW IN A WINDOW BOX

dill

lemon

parsley

onion

grilled mackerel

COD

pome-
granate
sauce

FISH + CHIPS

Potato churros with red pepper sauce

Makes 20, plus 300ml sauce	Preparation time: 30 minutes	Cooling time: 20 minutes	Cooking time: 40 minutes

When I was in Barcelona I visited a classic *churrería*, which felt like the local spot to gather, a bit like the local café where you would grab a builder's cup of tea and catch up with the latest gossip. It was cheap and cheerful, and they made sinfully good churros, served with rich hot chocolate so thick that you could stand them up in it. Although they are traditionally a breakfast food, if you switch an ingredient or two they make a great savoury dish.

For the potato churros

75g butter

100g potato flour

100g plain flour

1 tsp caster sugar

½ tsp sea salt

¼ tsp baking powder

2 eggs

1 litre sunflower or vegetable oil, for deep-frying

½ tsp sweet smoked paprika

For the red pepper sauce

4 red peppers

1 clove of garlic, peeled

1 tbsp extra virgin olive oil

6 cherry tomatoes

sea salt and freshly ground black pepper

Equipment

a piping bag with a 1cm star-shaped nozzle

Melt the butter in a medium saucepan, and when it starts to bubble gently beat in both of the flours, along with the sugar, salt and baking powder. Mix with a wooden spoon until it comes together, then crack in the eggs one by one, and mix again. Place the churros batter in a piping bag fitted with a star-shaped nozzle, and leave to chill in the fridge while you make the pepper sauce.

Preheat the grill to high. Cut the peppers in half and remove the seeds. Place skin side up on an oiled baking tray and grill for 15–20 minutes, or until blackened and tender. Place in a plastic bag and leave to steam for about 20 minutes.

When cool enough to handle, remove and discard the skins and place the flesh in a blender with the garlic, olive oil and tomatoes. Blitz until very smooth. Taste for seasoning.

Heat the sunflower oil in a large heavy-based pan on a high heat – you want it to reach 170°C. Test the temperature of the oil with a tiny amount of the batter. If it fizzes when it hits the oil, you are ready to start frying.

Pipe the batter out directly into the hot oil. Use a pair of scissors to snip each churro at the piping nozzle when it's about 10cm long. Fry the churros in two batches for 5–6 minutes, or until lightly pale golden. They will need to be turned carefully a few times with a long-handled slotted spoon.

Drain on paper towel. Sprinkle with a little smoked paprika while still hot, and serve with the red pepper sauce on the side.

Get ahead
The sauce can be made in advance, but the churros are best eaten hot from the fryer.

Homemade cottage cheese

Makes:
300g

Preparation time:
15 minutes

Resting time:
1 hour

Making your own cottage cheese might seem a little unnecessary but the homemade stuff is nothing like the shop-bought variety. It makes the perfect base for my English garden salad (see page 42).

2 litres whole milk

sea salt and freshly ground black pepper

juice of 4 lemons

In a large pan, heat the milk with a few grinds of salt and pepper. Just before it comes to the boil, take it off the heat. Stir in the lemon juice, then cover and set aside for 30 minutes. The milk will curdle and separate into whey and curd.

Pour through a sieve lined with a clean tea towel or muslin. Hang the tea towel over the sink for the curd to drain for around 30 minutes. When drained, twist the tea towel around the top of the cheese and squeeze it dry.

3 ways with cottage cheese

Chunky tomato cottage cheese

8 cherry tomatoes

300g cottage cheese

sea salt and freshly ground pepper

Finely chop the tomatoes. Season the cottage cheese with salt and pepper and place in a serving bowl. Scatter the tomatoes on top and serve with tortilla chips.

Herby cottage cheese

300g cottage cheese

8 tbsp crème fraîche or Greek yogurt

a small bunch of finely chopped chives or other herbs

a pinch of salt

½ tsp freshly ground pepper

Put the cheese into a large bowl and mix with the crème fraîche or yoghurt and the herbs. Season with the salt and pepper if desired.

Sweet and seedy cottage cheese

300g cottage cheese

6 tbsp Greek yogurt

4 tbsp mixed seeds (pumpkin, hemp, linseed, sesame), toasted

4 tbsp honey

Put the cheese into a large bowl and mix with the Greek yoghurt. In a separate bowl mix the toasted seeds with the honey. Divide the cheese mixture between 4 bowls and serve each with a dollop of the honey and seeds in the middle.

Tips

Cottage cheese can be flavoured with many different herbs and spices, such as chopped basil, parsley, coriander or sweet smoky paprika.

You can serve the sweet version with fresh fruit and granola.

Get ahead

Cottage cheese will keep for a couple of days in the fridge, in an airtight container.

Stock cubes

Makes:
14

Cooking time:
45 minutes

Preparation time:
2 minutes

Having good stock to hand means having a constant source of flavour to play with. But in a small kitchen it can be tricky to store fresh stock all the time. Reducing stock down until it's intensely concentrated, then freezing it in ice cube trays, is a great way of making it available for any occasion, without taking up too much precious space.

1 litre fresh ham stock (use the stock from the smoked ham hocks on page 93)

Equipment

a 14-hole ice cube tray

Place the stock in a large wide pan and simmer for around 45 minutes, or until reduced to about 200ml. Pour into an empty ice cube tray and leave to cool before placing in the freezer.

Tip
You can use this stock whenever you like; it's perfect for my speedy one-pot noodle (page 102).

Mayonnaise

Makes approx. 250ml

3 egg yolks, at room temperature

200–250ml sunflower or vegetable oil (you can replace 100–125ml with olive oil if you prefer a peppery taste)

2 tsp white wine vinegar or lemon juice

sea salt

Place the egg yolks in a large glass or stainless steel bowl set on a damp tea towel (to stop the bowl from slipping). Whisk the yolks a little, then add the oil drop by drop, whisking continuously, until the eggs begin to thicken and become pale. Continue drizzling the oil into the mixture until you have achieved the consistency you like. Add a few drops of white wine vinegar or lemon juice and season with salt.

To flavour your mayonnaise, stir in 1–2 tablespoons of harissa (to taste) for a spicy kick, or 1 tablespoon of lemon, orange or grapefruit zest for a zingy twist.

Tartare sauce

Makes approx. 270ml

1 tbsp each of chopped capers, chopped cornichons, chopped parsley, chopped tarragon and chopped chervil

1 quantity of mayonnaise, as above

Stir the capers, cornichons and herbs into the mayonnaise. Serve with snap, crackle and pop fish (see page 97).

Sweet chilli sauce

Makes about 400ml	Preparation time: 5 minutes	Cooking time: 15 minutes	Cooling time: 30 minutes

I have quite a collection of chilli sauces in my fridge, from the super-fiery stuff to this one, which you can pretty much put on anything if you fancy a sweet and spicy kick.

200g caster sugar

180ml white wine vinegar

3cm piece of ginger, peeled and finely chopped

3–4 small red chillies, very finely chopped, with seeds

1 tbsp cornflour

Place 200ml of water in a small saucepan with the sugar, vinegar, ginger and chillies on a high heat. Bring to the boil, then continue to boil for 10 minutes, stirring occasionally.

Whisk 1½ tablespoons of the liquid into the cornflour in a small bowl, then add back to the saucepan. Turn the heat down to low and cook for about 5 minutes, until it thickens to a just-pourable consistency, stirring continuously with a wooden spoon. Decant into sterilized jars and leave for around 30 minutes to cool completely.

Serve with the soft steamed buns on page 223.

Tip
Depending on the heat of the chillies and your personal preference, you can adjust the number used and remove the seeds if desired.

Get ahead
The sauce can be made ahead and decanted into sterilized jars.

To sterilize glass jars, wash thoroughly and drain upside down. Place on a tray in an oven at 180°C (fan) for 10 minutes. Sterilize the lids by placing in boiling water on the hob for 10 minutes, then remove carefully and leave to dry on clean tea towels.

Miso toffee cherry tomatoes

Makes
20

Preparation time:
10 minutes

Cooking time:
15 minutes

I love to play around with sweet and savoury flavours. I first tasted a version of this recipe in a French–Japanese restaurant in Nice. I loved the way this little appetizer looks. Very chic! The French name *tomates d'amour* ('love tomatoes') had me too. The miso adds a little saltiness to the caramel and works so well (just think salted butter caramel).

20 cherry tomatoes

2 tbsp furikake sprinkles* or a mix of white and black sesame seeds

2 tbsp sweet white miso paste

100ml hot water

300g caster sugar

Equipment

20 x 10cm bamboo skewers or toothpicks

a digital or sugar thermometer

A mix of black and white sesame seeds, seaweeds and dried shiso leaves. Found in Asian supermarkets or online.

Wash and dry the cherry tomatoes, then place one on each of the bamboo skewers. Put the furikake sprinkles or sesame seeds into a ramekin or small bowl, and line a baking tray with baking paper.

Dilute the miso paste in the hot water and place in a medium heavy-based saucepan on a medium heat. Add the sugar and allow to dissolve – do not stir, but swirl the pan around if needed. When the sugar has fully dissolved, simmer until it reaches 140°C and becomes a light rusty brown. Take off the heat.

Quickly submerge the skewered tomatoes completely into the caramel. Let the excess drip off before immediately dipping into the furikake or sesame seeds and placing on the baking paper. Leave to set for 5 minutes before eating.

Tips
Use a light-coloured pan as it's easier to see the colour of the caramel changing.

Don't wait too long before dipping the candied tomatoes into the sprinkles, otherwise they won't stick.

When cleaning your saucepan, put plenty of water in it and return to the heat; the caramel will dissolve and you can pour it away.

Get ahead
Don't make these more than a couple of hours in advance, as the toffee will soften with the humidity in the air.

large cocotte

large frying pan

speed
peeler

small pot

stainless steel
mixing bowls

heatproof
spatula

digital
scales

knives

Equipment

I've always believed that you don't need the latest gadgets and gizmos to make a delicious meal, and have often cooked in places where not everything is to hand. I've built up my kitchen equipment over the years, but if I had to do it all over again on a small budget these are the things I would initially invest in:

Large cocotte
Perfect for slow cooking dishes. Also great because you can transfer it from hob to oven. Not the cheapest item to buy, but a good-quality one will last you a lifetime. I've found a few that are in good nick at charity shops and flea markets.

Large frying pan
Invest in one with a heavy base (it conducts the heat better) and a good-quality handle (usually the first thing to break).

Small saucepan
For the smaller jobs where you don't need a large cocotte.

Speed peeler
One of my favourite tools, not because I love peeling potatoes but more because you can use it to make ribbons out of cucumbers, courgettes, carrots and many other things to jazz up your salad.

Small and large stainless steel or glass mixing bowls
Plastic bowls are harder to get super clean. They're more likely to have traces of grease from being used beforehand, which is the last thing you want when you're making a meringue. A spotless bowl is essential for making meringues and stainless steel or glass mixing bowls are perfect for this. They also come in handy for melting chocolate over a simmering pan of water.

A chef's knife, a serrated bread knife and a small vegetable knife, plus a knife sharpener
If there's one thing you should spend money on it's knives. Well looked after and kept sharp, they should last you at least a decade, if not a lifetime. Make sure to store your knives in a knife block or on a magnetic knife strip, not in a drawer.

Heatproof spatula
Better than a wooden spoon, a heatproof spatula (silicone is great) can scrape the sides and bottom of the saucepan to ensure nothing ends up burning. Can also double up for gently folding batter.

Digital scales
I used to teach French baking to American tourists in Paris and I was constantly trying to convince them that weighing ingredients is an absolute must when it comes to baking. So invest in one of these! It also comes in handy when measuring liquids (1ml = 1g), meaning no measuring jug is needed and you can be accurate to the decimal point.

Oven thermometer

I regularly end up using ovens in many different kitchens, and no matter what the thermometer says on the oven it is more often than not incorrect. Having an additional oven thermometer is a good way to make sure the temperature is correct for baking.

Whisk

When you're buying a whisk, look for one with sturdy metal 'spokes'. Flimsy ones mean it will take longer to whip up egg whites and cream.

Fine-meshed sieve

Doubles up for sifting lumps out of icing sugar or draining off liquids.

Springform baking tin

Probably the most popular size when it comes to baking is 20cm diameter. A springform with its easy release lever will limit the risk of cakes sticking to the sides.

Chopping board (wood or plastic)

If you want to take good care of your knives, make sure never to chop on a glass or marble surface. Don't drag the knife blade across the board to scrape ingredients into a pot, instead turn the blade upside down to scrape. Using the blade to scrape the board is the quickest way of blunting the blade.

Not a must but some additional favourites:

Japanese mandolin

Comes in handy for making equally thin sliced potatoes for your gratin. The grater blade for julienne vegetables makes the crunchiest slaw (rather than a soggy one). Just make sure to be careful and use the hand guard!

Microplane grater

Perfect for zesting citrus fruit as it only takes the fine layer of zest rather than the pith, and equally useful for finely grating hard cheeses.

Piping bag with a set of piping nozzles

If you're a budding baker, then a good piping bag (go for the silicone-coated ones which can be easily cleaned rather than the old-fashioned cloth ones) and a set of piping nozzles (star tip and round) are a must.

Containers

Whenever I use up a jar of jam or honey it gets washed out and used to store dry ingredients – it's much better than having open packets lying around. In addition to jam jars I also have a selection of good-quality airtight containers; perfect for storing leftovers in the fridge or freezing them.

Flat and angled spatulas

I have mini (12cm) spatulas, both angled and straight, as well as large ones. They make easy work of icing cakes and the larger ones are handy for moving cakes around. Also great for lifting up ingredients to see whether they're cooked underneath.

oven thermometer

whisk

sieve

springform
cake tin

chopping
board

piping bag
and nozzles

Japanese mandolin

microplane grater

knives

Chilli sauce

Eggs

Butter

Cheese

Tinned cherry
tomatoes

Puy or beluga
lentils

fresh herbs

Flaky sea salt

Wine vinegar

Cook's Notes & Ingredients

This is a little glimpse into my fridge and kitchen cupboards. You'll always find these ingredients hanging about, even if I haven't been for a recent grocery shop.

Eggs

I love eggs whether they're fried, poached or soft boiled; hence me splashing out a little more for eggs with a rich yolk. You can see the difference when you make a pastry cream (such as for the rhubarb and custard millefeuille on page 188) as it will have a richer yellow hue, making it more appetizing. For me, a fried egg served sunnyside up will immediately brighten up even the dullest grey winter's day.

The recipes in this book were made using medium free-range (and organic) eggs. I tend to keep them at room temperature in my kitchen as I get through them quickly and it makes them less likely to crack when boiling them for a soft-boiled egg. For baking also, it is handy to have all your ingredients at room temperature when you start.

Butter

My mantra 'Butter makes everything better' stems from my Austrian grandma's love of the golden stuff. I don't need to say much about how adding a knob of butter to a dish will give it a smooth taste. You can even try your hand at making your own on page 239.

Cheese

To say I love cheese is an understatement. I have a serious problem. There's always a piece of cheese (preferably the pungent kind) in my fridge. Paired with a few cornichons or pickled onions and some crackers, it's the lazy, but delicious, dinner I turn to when I've been cooking all day.

Crème fraîche (or thick Greek yoghurt for the lighter days)

A versatile ingredient: a simple blob of the creamy stuff with some fresh berries, a drizzle of melted chocolate and dessert is sorted. Also perfect for salad dressings, adding to soups or making sauces.

Salt

For seasoning I always use a flaky sea salt such as Maldon.

Meat

Always buy the best quality meat you can afford. I would prefer not to eat it if I am unsure of how it was raised, so I try hard to source mine from trustworthy suppliers. I am also a big fan of slow-cooking cuts and offal, which are tastier in my opinion and far more affordable that chicken breasts or fillets of beef. Turner and George (www.turnerandgeorge.co.uk) are an excellent source of all things carnivorous, and they deliver across the UK.

Fish

I am fortunate to have access to an excellent local fishmonger that only sells fish caught in a sustainable manner. Don't be afraid to ask your fishmonger where the fish comes from and look out for the seal of approval from the MCS or the RSPCA Freedom Food scheme if you are buying tinned or frozen fish.

Fresh herbs

Even living in the city I still have a window box or two with plenty of herbs and the odd radish growing in it. It's much cheaper and significantly more rewarding than buying them. Before the cold winter hits your harvest, pop your herbs in the freezer.

Wine vinegar

I prefer to dress my salads with red or white wine vinegar, rather than balsamic, which can be overbearingly sweet and sticky. Wine vinegar has a cleaner taste. I also use it in sauces to add a of bit acidity when needed, such as in my summer spaghetti bolognese sauce on page 135 or my chilled cucumber soup on page 53.

Chilli sauce

I have at least three types of chilli sauce in my fridge: a sweet one (perfect for dipping spring rolls, like my own chilli sauce on page 251), a fiery one (I love spicy food and will often use chilli sauce like a kid would liberally use tomato ketchup) and Tabasco – perfect for seasoning a bloody mary.

Tinned cherry tomatoes

Sweeter and more flavourful than their plum cousins. I've used them in quite a few recipes, such as my cream of tomato soup on page 18 or the seafood chilli on page 94.

Lentils – Puy or beluga

I always feel a little virtuous when I eat lentils, unlike with pasta or potatoes. You might call me a lentil snob as I prefer the slightly more expensive type, but both Puy and beluga hold their shape better and have a delicious nutty flavour.

Oven

I use the fan setting for most of my cooking as I find that the heat distributes more evenly. If you have a conventional oven then add 20°C to the temperature. It is helpful to keep a thermometer for precision.

Cook's Notes

Space to add your own scribbles and doodles

Index

Page references in **bold** indicate photographs

v indicates a vegetarian recipe

gf indicates a gluten-free recipe

Acknowledgements

Thank you!

Like the old saying 'behind every successful man is a strong woman' goes, a similar thing could be said about a successful food writer. Behind the scenes there is a brilliant team of people who support my writing and ensure the book is the best it can be. Without these people there would be no book. So a BIG thank you to:

my publisher: Penguin and the fantastic team at Michael Joseph

my editors: Lindsey Evans and Tamsin English

my art director: John Hamilton

my photographer: David Loftus

my food stylist: Frankie Unsworth

my prop stylists: Lydia Brun and Olivia Wardle

my literary agent: Lizzy Kremer, Harriet Moore and the team at David Higham

my assistants and recipe tester:
Libby Davis, Helen Vass,
Charlie Phillips and Bren Parkins-Knight

And last but not least my friends, family and Robert Wiktorin.

And the following brands
for the lovely clothes:

Petit Bateau
www.petit-bateau.co.uk

Mrs Pomeranz
www.mrs-pomeranz.com

And the following shops and brands for
lending us some beautiful props:

Rockett St George
www.rockettstgeorge.co.uk

The Deli Downstairs
www.thedelidownstairs.co.uk

Fired Earth
(special thanks to Elizabeth of Mar)
Most of the Fired Earth tiles used for
the purpose of this shoot are wall tiles
and not suitable for surfaces. For more
info on their tiles, please visit the
Fired Earth website.
www.firedearth.com

Present and Correct
(special thanks to Neal)
www.presentandcorrect.com

Le Creuset
www.lecreuset.co.uk

The Salvation Army
www.salvationarmy.org.uk

Anthropologie
www.anthropologie.eu

Leila's general store
www.leilasgeneralstore.com

Julia Smith ceramics
www.juliasmithceramics.com